.

Endorsements

Few things are as impactful as a prophetic word wrapped in God's Word. Too often we hear from leaders too heavy on one and too light on the other. This is not so with LaJun and Valora's revelation. They have heard a word from Heaven and pushed it relentlessly through the filter of Scripture—proving it, testing it, and now boldly declaring it with promise. Not only is the teaching sound, their Suddenly Confessions, Declarations, Prayer, and Scriptures are a powerful, practical process through which to apply this prophetic word to bear fruit in your own life. Open the pages and discover your suddenly season…

Wendy K. Walters
Master Coach, Motivational Speaker, President of
The Favor Foundation
www.wendykwalters.com

LaJun Cole, Sr and Valora Shaw-Cole have a passion for God that overflows into their teaching and international ministry. These dual apostolic and prophetic gifts to the Body of Christ have written a book that is so timely needed today in the 21st century. *Sudden Breakthrough* carries a strong Issachar prophetic anointing to help the reader come into their due season of acceleration, reconciliation, and restitution of all things. This book serves as a prophetic catalyst that will inspire, equip, and propel leaders and readers alike to know and understand their *kairos* season, which I believe is the "suddenly" season of God. As modern day apostles and prophets, the Coles' possess a wealth of experience, knowledge, and prophetic insight in positioning leaders and believers strategically to possess the promises of the Lord for their lives. After reading this thought-provoking book, I couldn't put it down because it awakened the "sleeping giant" on the inside of me. *Sudden Breakthrough* becomes the reader's personal prophet, journal, and Holy Spirit GPS that will navigate and order your steps in Christ. I fully endorse the powerful message contained in this book. Each chapter has the prophetic release to activate the "omega anointing" to finish the race of destiny. I highly recommend this book to every believer ready to breakthrough life barriers, strongholds, and invisible restrictions. This book is a prophetic anthem for the believer to boldly declare, "It's My Suddenly Season!"

Dr. Hakeem Collins
Founder, Champions International
Author of *Heaven Declares, Prophetic Breakthrough*
and *Command Your Healing*

From the first word to the last, this book will immerse you in a prophetic teaching, promise, and activation that flows directly to you from the Spirit of God. This book, without a doubt, is a NOW word! Don't miss out on its contents! As you read the pages, you will find yourself leaning into each and every statement and illustration. Your faith will rise up to lay hold of your season of SUDDENLIES in all the realms of life. Be blessed and encouraged as you peruse the pages, make the confessions, and meditate on the prophetic promises being presented to you. I highly recommend this book.

Jennifer Eivaz
Executive Pastor, Harvest Christian Center Turlock CA and Founder of Harvest Ministries International
Author, *The Intercessors Handbook* and *Seeing the Supernatural*

If you want to experience a suddenly moment in your life, this book is sure to stir and activate that moment for you. This book demonstrates how GOD moves suddenly, by taking a moment to turn your life around for His glory. You can feel the excitement, expectation, and experience from the authors that suddenly is possible, and how GOD can take your worst days by turning them into your best days. This book is a page-turner and will bless you from the beginning to the end. I highly recommend this book.

Sophia Ruffin
Founder of Sophia Ruffin Ministries
Author of best-seller *From Point Guard to Prophet*

As America's #1 Confidence Coach, I have encircled the globe several times. In all my travels, I've never met anyone who didn't need the confidence to go to their next level. My good friends, La Jun and Valora Cole, have penned a masterpiece, which is sure to do just that. Each page infuses you with the faith and confidence you need to access your next level of Suddenlies and Sudden Breakthroughs. I highly recommend this book.

Dr. Keith Johnson
America's #1 Confidence Coach
Founder and CEO, Keith Johnson International and Destiny College International
Author of Amazon's best-sellers *The Confidence Solution, LQ Solution,* and *Confidence for Living Wealthy*
www.keithjohnson.tv

Sudden Breakthrough

Sudden Breakthrough

Decrees, Prayers, and Confessions to Access Your Suddenly Moment

LaJun M. Cole, Sr. and Valora Shaw-Cole

DESTINY IMAGE® PUBLISHERS, INC.

P.O. Box 310, Shippensburg, PA 17257-0310

"Promoting Inspired Lives."

This book and all other Destiny Image and Destiny Image Fiction books are available at Christian bookstores and distributors worldwide.

Cover design by Eileen Rockwell

For more information on foreign distributors, call 717-532-3040.

Reach us on the Internet: www.destinyimage.com.

ISBN 13 TP: 978-0-7684-4358-5
ISBN 13 eBook: 978-0-7684-4359-2
ISBN 13 HC: 978-0-7684-4361-5
ISBN 13 LP: 978-0-7684-4360-8

For Worldwide Distribution, Printed in the U.S.A.

1 2 3 4 5 6 7 8 / 22 21 20 19 18

Acknowledgements

WE BELIEVE THAT appreciation is a key to sustained success in any endeavor. One thing we have learned along our journey is that people don't have to do anything for you, but when they do it's important to appreciate them.

We want to thank God first, for counting us faithful despite our humanity and trusting us with this amazing revelation of Suddenly.

Next, we want to thank our pastor and spiritual father Apostle John Eckhardt for pushing us to write this book and for believing in us. It was during the Reset Conference in Houston that we were on Periscope and teaching a series entitled "Hearing the Voice of God" that we received the revelation that God was going to answer our prayers and that He would do it Suddenly.

We are proud to acknowledge our son, Antoine J. L. Cole and our sister Kaiesha MaGruder for their contributions and support. We would also like to thank the members of the church, which God chose us to birth and pastor, Perfected Love International Fellowship, and our sons and daughters in ministry, which we call simply, "The Coalition." Finally, we would like to thank our Facebook and Periscope family for pushing us. On the third day of our

Midnight Cry Prayer scope, we began to deal with the topic of "It's My Suddenly Season." Our intent was to teach on the subject that day and on that day only, and then transition to the next subject the following day. However, the next day during the broadcast, as I gave the new subject many of the viewers began to write, "It's My Suddenly Season." It was on that day that this book was conceived, and thirty days later, it was birthed. Ladies and gentlemen, you are the reason that this book is being birthed, so thank you so much for stretching us and putting a demand on our anointing. Lastly, but certainly not least, we want to thank Destiny Image Publishers for seeing potential in the message of Suddenly and publishing *Sudden Breakthrough.*

Contents

Prophetic Release
I Am the God of the Suddenlies

SONS AND DAUGHTERS, many of you have been believing and waiting on Me to release things suddenly in your life. For some, it has appeared that you have been forgotten or that your prayers have been held up. I have come to tell you today that I have not forgotten you and this is your season for answered prayers. This is the time that chronological time meets my Kairos time and as they collide, you will experience the breakthrough you have desired and sought Me for. I am releasing Suddenly breakthroughs in every area of your life.

I am releasing Suddenly breakthroughs in your mind, your will, your emotions, your faith, your vision, and in every area of your life. You will not see things as you have seen them before, you will see with new eyes—eyes which view things according to My pattern and My faith and My heart's desire for you and the life I designed for you to live from the beginning. I am changing your perspective; as your perspective changes, your circumstances will change. My Glory is going to be revealed in your life like never before. You can expect to receive the manifestation of the things you have been believing for and asking for in the season. I have declared that this is your Suddenly Season. You will go to sleep one night in one situation and wake up the next morning in your next dimension. I have anointed you for great things, no matter what your current situation may be. I have not called you to remain in your current state. It is only a place of transition because in your Suddenly Season, things are subject to change at any moment. Do not confess and declare what you see but rather confess and declare what you are believing Me for.

Your confessions and declarations of faith will release the angels to move on your behalf. Your confession of faith will cause the earth to align with My heavenly plan for your life. You shall decree a thing and it shall be established in this season. Remember not the former things because I am doing a new thing in your life and I am doing it SUDDENLY! Get ready to receive it! Posture and position yourself to receive all that you have been believing Me for; because when your Suddenly Season arrives, you will not have time to get prepared, you must be ready to move forward. In this season, I am moving quickly. So, get ready and receive your Suddenly because I am the God of SUDDEN BREAKTHROUGH.

Introduction

The Year of Fulfillment, Suddenlies, and Sudden Breakthrough

EACH YEAR, GOD gives our local church a prophetic word to guide us through the year. In 2017, God spoke to us that it was the Year of Fulfillment and Suddenlies. We believe that this word when embraced will begin to release sudden breakthroughs in the life of the person who believes, embraces, and confesses it.

This is the Year of Fulfillment of My Word and prophetic promises in your life. It will happen Suddenly!

The word "suddenly" literally means quickly or unexpectant. Some of its synonyms are immediately, instantaneously, straightway, suddenly, promptly, abruptly, and swiftly, without warning, out of the blue, without notice.

He went on to tell us that this was the year that He was fulfilling every prophetic word, which He had sent to us. He said everything that we went through was all for our preparation to bring us to this place and season of our lives. Nothing would be wasted, not one of our tears or the pain and the heartache we experienced would be for naught.

While reading Acts 2, we noticed how the challenges the early church encountered after Christ's ascension, literally positioned them in the upper room. The important factor was not just that they were positioned in the upper room but more so that they were postured for Suddenlies to happen.

> *And when the day of Pentecost was fully come, they were all with one accord in one place. And suddenly there came a sound from heaven as of a rushing mighty wind, and it filled all the house where they were sitting.*
>
> Acts 2:1-2 (KJ21)

Notice in verse 1 that they were all together in one place and they were on one accord. Suddenlies happen where there is unity. The key ingredient to their suddenly was not that they were positioned in a certain place but more so that they were postured for Suddenly breakthrough and that is exactly what they received.

Acts 1:6-8 shares with us that Christ had promised the disciples the manifestation of His Spirit, which would empower them to fulfill their assignment in the earth.

> *So when they had come together, they asked Him, "Lord, will You at this time restore the kingdom to Israel? He said to them, "It is*

not for you to know the times or the dates, which the Father has fixed by His own authority. But you shall receive power when the Holy Spirit comes upon you. And you shall be My witnesses in Jerusalem, and in all Judea and Samaria, and to the ends of the earth."

Acts 1:6-8 (MEV)

Each of us have received precious promises from God, which we are waiting to see manifestation of. What we must know and rest assured of is that when He promises us something He will perform it. He declares He is not a man that He should lie, neither is He the son of a man that He should repent, for if He said it shall He not do it and if He spoke it shall He not make it good. Grasping this understanding of the immutability (unchangeable nature) of God can revolutionize our thinking and our faithful walk, which will cause us to be positioned and postured to receive the Suddenlies of God in our life.

***

This is the season that God is manifesting and bringing to fruition every prophetic word and promise, which He has made to us. He loves you with an unquenchable love and nothing can separate you from His love. He says that it is His good pleasure to give us the Kingdom and that there is no good thing that He will withhold from them that love Him and walk uprightly. Likewise, His Word declares that if we delight ourselves in Him, He promises to give us the desires of our hearts. With this in mind, we must have complete trust that whatever He declares or speaks for us, He will bring to pass. In this season of your life, make up your mind that you are determined to receive all that God has for you.

Believing for a "Suddenly"
by John Eckhardt

Prayer

Tonight, we ask you Lord as we gather here that you would do something special and something unusual. Something Lord that will cause us to be launched into another realm of victory, favor, and breakthrough. Let no one that has come to this meeting tonight be disappointed, but Lord meet their expectation by your Spirit and by your anointing. Lord you know what everyone needs, and you know where everyone of us are on our journey. Give us everything we need to move forward during this midyear service. In the middle of the year strengthen us and bless us, increase us to finish strong in 2017. Lord release miracles, breakthroughs, and favor upon everyone that walks in this building. Let our lives change from glory to glory, from favor to favor, and from strength to strength. Lord, let a divine suddenly hit our lives, let there be a suddenly for everyone that has come to this suddenly conference, do something suddenly in our lives. We believe you for it, we ask you for it, release our faith for it, we bless you for it, and we praise you for it. In Jesus name, amen.

Somebody shout SUDDENLY! One more time Suddenly!

Believe God for Faith for Suddenlies

I don't think that Suddenly is just a nice title for a conference. That's a word that God gave La Jun and Valora Cole.

Often you go to conferences and they say, Signs, Wonders, and Miracles and the only sign is the sign on the door and no one gets healed, it's just a nice slogan and title. I don't believe we should have meetings with just a nice title. I believe we should have meetings where the manifestation of the title happens in our life. How many people are believing God for a suddenly in your life? How many of you need a suddenly in your life? You need something sudden to happen, quickly, immediately, straightway. One word can turn your life around. One word can make the difference.

I believe I have a word from the Lord for you tonight. I'm going to talk about Faith for Suddenlies tonight. I am really sensing this that God always is attracted to faith. Say it with me. God is always attracted to faith, faith gets Gods attention, faith causes God to move. Even when Jesus told the woman, I cannot take the children's bread and give it to dogs. Most of us would have turned around offended because He called you a dog. But she said even the dogs, you are talking about being a comeback kid, she had a comeback for Jesus. When you can come back on Jesus, you are tough. She said even the dogs eat the breadcrumbs. Jesus thought, this is a tough girl here I have to give you what you want. Cause when Jesus spoke, everybody shut up. Usually when Jesus spoke, it was the last word. But when He said I cannot give the children's bread to dogs, she said, "I don't want the bread I want a crumb." I believe even just a crumb can get me delivered. I don't need the whole loaf give me a crumb. I will take what the others don't want. Sometimes people don't want certain things and you have to get the leftovers. You can get a miracle in the leftovers that others didn't want, so just give me the leftovers. I'll take the crumb and I'll take the leftovers. So because of her faith Jesus performs a Suddenly. Jesus said, I have not seen so great a faith. And to top it all off, she was a Gentile. Faith moves God, faith gets God's attention, Faith for anything in the word will cause you to receive and I'm finding out that when you begin to study certain subjects in Scripture such as favor, and you study every Scripture on favor. Your faith begins to be increased for favor and because of your faith for favor, you receive it. A lot of believers are not believing God for favor because they have never heard about favor. Faith comes by what? Hearing and so whatever you hear is what you will have faith for. So, it's important for us to preach certain things that we ordinarily don't preach. So, when I heard this word Suddenly that they received. I've studied Suddenly before and I heard that word suddenly before, but I haven't really extensively studied it. I said to myself, "Is it possible to believe God and to have faith for Suddenlies" just like you have faith for favor. If suddenly is in Scripture, can we have faith to believe God for some Suddenlies? And the Lord said, yes! The Lord said, "tell my people to believe me for some Suddenlies." How many people need some Suddenlies? A suddenly comes quickly, and some of us have been waiting on God for over 150 years or so it seems and you need a sudden miracle, you need a sudden breakthrough, you've been coming to church shouting and dancing for years and years and years and it looks like nothing is happening but I'm here to let you know that there is a suddenly that God is about to release in your life. You've been waiting, you've been praying, you've been believing, but I want you to believe God for the faith to receive the suddenly today. I don't care how slow it's been. Tell someone *believe God for a suddenly to hit your life*. Tell someone else, *Believe God for a Suddenly to hit your life. I want to share some things with you tonight about Suddenly.*

I believe tonight God wants your faith to come alive and I believe one of the areas He wants your faith to come alive in is in the area of Suddenlies. Sometimes in life, you could be living year after year and nothing major ever really happens in your life. You hear testimonies of other people who received sudden breakthroughs and sudden miracles. Let me give you an example. In my church, I was preaching on the subject of thousands, and I stood up one Sunday and I began to prophecy about thousands. I prophesied to the people that thousands were going to hit some of their bank accounts. As soon as I said it, I thought to myself, "Lord I hope this happens." Have you ever given a prophecy and it's so big and you wonder, "God, why did I say that"? But you felt such a strong unction that you said it anyway. In those instances, God has to move you to say it because He knows you're not going to say it without an unction. And you are so stirred up that you say it, then after you say it, you realize what you just said. Then a few weeks later, I had a member come into my office and say pastor here is the prophecy that you released. She said I have a check for you, it's a tithe of what hit my bank account. It wasn't a 1,000-dollar check, it wasn't a 5,000-dollar check, it wasn't a 10,000-dollar check, it wasn't a 20,000-dollar check. It was a 50,000-dollar check. It was a tithe of the half a million dollars which hit her bank account. If you want your pastor to have a good

Sunday, hand him a 50,000-dollar check. I guarantee you, I don't care what he or she is going through, the joy of the Lord will be his strength that day. The reason the money hit her account because it was a suddenly. Her husband had written some music years before; and as a result they used his music in a movie, which produced millions of dollars. She said she had no idea that they had even used his music in the movie until she received the check for half a million dollars and as a result she gave a tithe of it to our church. God is releasing sudden financial blessings and breakthroughs.

Suddenly God is releasing a Revival of Favor

Boom, it was a suddenly! So when I heard the word suddenly that the Coles had been ministering at 1:00 p.m. and Midnight every day, teaching and ministering on the word suddenly. I know that if you hear that word, embrace it and believe it, that it can bring tremendous blessings. When I got up the other day, I heard the word Revival of Favor. I don't really like to use the word revival because it has become so religious. I generally never call a meeting revival. There is nothing wrong with it because it is biblical, but people have used it religiously and during every revival the same people get saved. It is like you see the people who just got saved for the twelfth time every year in the revival. The preacher comes in and preaches the revival and immediately after the meeting the church goes back dead again. It wasn't a real revival because a real revival wakes you up and stirs you up and a real revival has humility and repentance attached. People begin to confess and get delivered and people begin to make amends with each other and are going to each other and apologizing for their actions, this is real revival. Revival is not the same people running around the church and running and jumping but not coming out of sin and not getting deliverance from the things that have had them bound. They just have an emotional revival. Real revival means something changes and people start walking and talking with each other again and getting free. So this is why I don't generally use the word revival. But I heard the word Revival of Favor. I not only want to give you a Revival of Favor I want to revive favor in your life. I want to cause favor to come alive in your life. I want to cause favor that has died, I want to cause favor that you have lost to come back again. Have you ever lost something, and you need restoration? The Lord said, tell my people, I want them to experience a Revival of Favor and then I heard Him say there is a wind of favor coming. The breath of God is coming and just like the wind blew upon the dry bones in the valley. The favor of God is going to blow on your life and every dry dead place in your life where you did not have favor. Get ready for it to come alive, your finances, your family, your marriage, your ministry, whatever you put your hands to. Somebody say Favor! Sometimes you hear these unusual words, you wake up and you have an unusual word that you never heard before. Because one word, one rhema word can change your life. If a word comes from God, it brings such tremendous release. I'm talking about a word, which proceeds out of the mouth of God. You can hear all kinds of sermons on Sunday but it's not always rhema. It's just somebody up talking from Scripture but it's not rhema. But when you hear that rhema, something quickens inside of you and you say, "My God I feel it something shifted!" It's not just somebody up quoting Scriptures. The Letter kills but the Spirit causes the spirit to come alive. Thank God for rhemas. So Lord let your rhema come into my life. Because a rhema word is a life-giving word that turns your life around. It's a word that breaks you free. You hear the word favor, you hear the word suddenly. You hear these unusual words. So when they begin to happen don't just say, "Oh, that's nice they are talking about suddenly. No, grab that word, receive the word, then begin to confess the word, begin to walk in the word. Why does God want to give the word Suddenly? Because there are some suddenly things He's ready to do in your life. He knows you need something quick. He knows you need something suddenly. He knows you've been going for years and years and years at the same pace but now He wants to hit you with a suddenly anointing that will shift you quickly into another level. Somebody shout Suddenly in this place.

When I heard them speak of this word I began to do a study on Suddenly because I believe sometimes in Scripture there are words we have not fully studied, and I believe we don't fully have an understanding of the word because we've not taken time to study it. We've not really looked at every Scripture and gotten or received a comprehensive understanding of a particular word. I believe there are subjects in Scripture that when God gives them to you, if you will spend time studying them God will give you a greater revelation of them. I've said this before that God fascinates me. I am fascinated by God. I don't know how anyone gets bored with God. God is the most fascinating person in the universe. God amazes me. I'm always learning something new about Him. I'm entering into my 40th year of preaching and I am still learning things that get me so excited until I say wow. I'm not going to be one of these saints that think they know everything. They come to service and sleep all service because they have heard all the best preachers. They have heard all the best choirs and they've been to every kind of meeting. They've been to every kind of seminar. They have heard the best of the best.

I am amazed at what I see in the area of suddenly. Just when you think you know God. He shows you another part of Him. I believe that throughout eternity. I was thinking that if we go to heaven and spend billions of years in heaven, what is there to do? Have you ever thought about this? Some people are just happy with getting to heaven and not going to hell. They say I'm not trying to figure out what will happen I just don't want to go to hell. We will figure that part out when we get there. I don't care if I float around on a cloud for a billion years I just want to get there. I'd just rather be bored in heaven than tormented in hell so I really don't care. Could it be that we will be learning about God for eternity Could it be that we will be learning about God for an eternity? Could it be that God is that deep? That God is that unsearchable? Until you can study Him for eternity and never exhaust. Tell someone God is big and God is unsearchable. Don't ever think you know everything about God because I believe that throughout eternity we will be fascinated about God. I think that's what makes life fascinating. I think one of the worst things that can happen is when you are bored. Have you ever been bored?

God is a God of Sudden surprises

I began to study the word Suddenly and I researched the word straightway, which is often used in the Book of Mark, the word straightway is used 42 times in the King James Version (KJV). The word immediately is used 55 times in the KJV and the word Suddenly is used 49 times. I asked God why is this word suddenly and straightway, immediately used so many times in Scripture? What are you trying to show me about suddenly, straightway, and immediately? The Lord began to show me some things. He said tell my people, "I like to do things Suddenly, because I like to surprise them." I don't think you got it. God said tell my people I am a God of surprises! Because when something happens Suddenly, it catches you off guard. All of a sudden it comes so quickly that sometimes you're not ready for it. God said tell my people to believe me for some surprises. I'm about to do some surprises in your life that you have not been expecting, it's going to hit your house, your finances, your ministry, and your life. Suddenly is about to surprise you. The Lord said tell them, it's going to be a good surprise, not a bad surprise but a good surprise. Tell somebody to get ready for some good surprises. I remember years ago in our church, we had a financial confession where we would confess that we were going to receive gifts and surprises. When you are not expecting stuff and it just happens. When someone just walks up and hands you a 50,000-dollar check out of nowhere. And tells you the Lord told me just to bless you.

That's a surprise. When someone just takes you out and says, "The Lord told me to buy you a car, which one do you want?" "When someone says I need to take you shopping and buy you some clothes so pick out what you want." That's a surprise. When someone just comes and hands you some property and says, "The Lord told me to sign this over to you." That's a surprise! Tell somebody to get ready for some surprises. God loves surprising His people. Just like you love surprising your children with good things. You tell your child, "I have something for you, I brought something for you." And they say, "What daddy?" and you say, "It's a surprise here you go!" That's the way our Father is.

Lord, How do I access your Suddenlies?

I then began to look at the Suddenlies in Scripture and I said Lord, show me how we can receive surprises from you? Is there something we can do that releases Suddenlies? Because when I study a subject I really want to gain an understanding of it. So I asked God what can we do to experience Suddenlies. What can we do that will release the Suddenlies of God into our life? The Lord took me to the story of Paul and Silas in jail where they prayed and sang praises unto God and suddenly there was an earthquake and the jails were open. God said tell my people that if they pray and praise me, I will do some Suddenlies in their life. How many of you have been praying and praising. Say it with me, "Prayer and Praise releases God's Suddenlies." I asked God, You mean to tell me that if I pray and praise you like Paul and Silas, I can receive a suddenly? And God said "Yes" The combination of prayer and praise, prayer and praise, prayer and praise will produce a suddenly. Pray, praise, pray, praise, pray and praise and Suddenly! Say it with me pray, praise, pray, praise, pray and praise then Suddenly. Say it one more time, "Pray, Praise, Pray, Praise, Pray, Praise, Suddenly!" Your prayers are not in vain, your praise is not in vain. I don't care what is going on, even if you're in the worst condition of your life. It doesn't matter how messed up the situation is, if you will pray and praise, God will send a suddenly and bring you out of any situation you may find yourself in.

That's why prayer and praise are exactly what the devil attempts to shut down when you are in trouble. You stop praying because you don't feel like praying, then you stop praising God. Everybody around you is standing and shouting praising God and you are sitting there thinking I will be glad when these folks sit down. You start to speak negative about other believers. You find yourself saying things like, "She always has to run, these people get on my nerves". Every church has that one person where no matter what they always have to run. And in your mind, you're like I hope you sit down somewhere. I'm tired of you running."

Prayer and Praise release the Suddenlies of God

I said to the Lord teach me about your Suddenlies and He said Prayer and Praise. Then He took me to the woman with the issue of blood. She had been bleeding for 12 years. She presses through the crowd and touched the hem of Jesus's garment and the Bible says immediately her blood flow stopped. The Lord said tell my people this, "If they learn how to press in faith they can receive a suddenly. Tell somebody, "Press in faith and it will bring a suddenly into your life." Faith and pressing through everything that told her to stop, everything that told her, "You can't get it" she just wouldn't stop. She kept pressing through and she said in her heart, "I don't need Him to lay hands on me, I don't need Him to pray for me, I don't need him to stop, I don't need Him to speak over me, but if I can just touch Him, I believe there is enough healing in His clothes to stop my blood from flowing." And when she touched Him, Jesus said, "Who touched Me?" The disciples said, "All these folks are touching you." And Jesus said, "No somebody pulled something out of Me." Then He told the woman, "Your faith has made you whole. Your faith has brought a Suddenly into your life." Tell somebody, "Faith will bring a Suddenly into your life." Faith will bring a suddenly into your life. Then the Lord took me to Jesus, Jesus ministry is a suddenly ministry because when you read the Gospels you see Jesus when He is born, then when He is 12 years old, He is in the temple right? Do you notice that for 18 years you don't see anything else? He shows up all of a sudden, gets baptized, and immediately He comes out of the water and the Spirit of God comes on Him. The Scripture says immediately the Spirit of God drives Him into the wilderness. Suddenly, He is going into the wilderness. The Lord said, "son tell my people that when My spirit comes on them, it will cause them to do some sudden things." Listen to me, a suddenly is not just when you receive a suddenly, sometimes it's when you do something suddenly. Sometimes God's anointing comes on you and you can't operate the same way, you have to step out of the boat and walk on the water. You have to get up and begin to move. You can't sit down and think about it and sit down and wait a couple years. When the anointing of God comes on your life, it's time to shift and move. There's a suddenly season that will come on your teaching, your preaching, your moving. God is going to raise up people suddenly. He is going to put His anointing on people that nobody has heard about. All the big shots on the platform but there is somebody who has been waiting on God and a new anointing is going to come on your life and suddenly you are going to go up in the spirit and suddenly you are going to be seen and suddenly you going to begin to walk in your ministry. Repeat after me, "Lord Let your spirit come upon me, and Lord let me walk in the suddenly." That's the anointing! How many people know that when the anointing gets on you, you will have to move. You have to do it quickly, amen! You have to move suddenly! I love when the anointing comes on an individual, they can't sit around titling their thumbs and waiting. When the anointing comes on you brother, you have to suddenly do something.

Paul the apostle encounters God suddenly

Then the Lord took me to the Book of Acts and I read Paul's encounter with Jesus. It says that suddenly there was a light from heaven that shined upon Paul. So Paul is on his way to Damascus, he is about to kill Christians and put them in prison. This was his daily routine. But he encountered a suddenly. The Lord told me to tell you, "Tell my people to get ready for some Suddenly encounters with me." Because this suddenly encounter turned Paul's life around. When Paul got blinded, for three days it said straightway, he preached that Jesus was the Christ. Can you imagine the church saying this is the man who is persecuting us. This is the man we are hiding from. And now he's preaching, so some of them didn't even trust him. They thought it was a trick. They didn't believe that it could happen, but God can do some Suddenlies. God can turn a drug addict around suddenly. God can turn a homosexual around suddenly! God can turn a drug dealer around suddenly. Let's pray that God would suddenly save your children, your grandchildren, your great grandchildren. The drug dealer, the alcoholic, and whoever it is that they would have a suddenly encounter. And when you have a suddenly encounter, your life suddenly changes. I like suddenly salvations when someone suddenly encounters the light of God coming on them. The Lord said, "Do you want some Suddenlies in your life?" I said, "Yes Lord." He said to me, "Pray, Praise, Press in faith, and let the Glory come on your life." That's what happened to Paul. The light, the glory of God shined from heaven and blinded him. The lord said, "If you want some Suddenlies, get in the Glory, get into a church that has the glory. Don't hang out in a place where there is no presence." Get around the Glory of God, Get around people that know how to worship, get around a place of my presence, let the Glory of God come on you. Because when you encounter God's Glory, God's Glory will cause some Suddenlies to come alive in your life. When you get the understanding that you can pray, you can praise, you can press in faith and when His glory shines on your life it produces Suddenlies. That's why I love the glory of God because when you get in the glory, get ready for some miracles. Do not attend a dead church where there is no glory, no power, and no anointing. You have to find somewhere where the Glory of God is and it makes you get on your face, it makes you bow down. It knocked Paul down to the ground. There is such a glory that comes, where you can't even stand anymore. You can't be cute in service, you have to get on your face and worship God because of the weight of His Glory and the cloud of His glory. When that cloud comes on your life, get ready for some Suddenlies. How many people want some Suddenlies? How many people want some surprises?

How do I get them? We can talk about this all day. Many are asking, "How do I get this? I don't want to just hear about it. I want this. What's the dynamic of it? How does it work? Lord give me understanding.

Israel is suddenly released from Egypt

Then the Lord showed me another way you can get a suddenly. He took me to Israel. They are in Egypt for 400 years. Moses shows up and begins to release miracles and judgments. But at the end, God told them this. He said, "Get ready to leave Egypt tonight. "Suddenly, although you have been here 400 years but tonight, you're coming out. He said, "Put your shoes on, get your clothes ready and when you eat this Passover meal, I'm going to do something in Egypt, I'm going to kill the first born and your coming out of here suddenly. And then the Scripture says that God gave them favor with the Egyptians and they spoiled the Egyptians. In other words, you are coming out tonight and you're not coming out broke, you are coming out with some resources. But it's going to be something suddenly.

I asked the Lord again, "What's the key to this?" and He said, "They had a Moses." Hosea 12: 13 says, "By a prophet, the Lord delivered Israel out of Egypt and by a Prophet was he preserved." The Lord said you can get around certain kinds of anointings and when you get around real prophets and real apostles and they begin to minister to you they can help you come into some Suddenlies. You can be bound for years and you get around the right anointing and brother they can speak one word over your life and suddenly your ministry breaks open. Amen, a man or woman of God can lay hands on you and suddenly God does something. You can get into one service under the anointing and suddenly something breaks open for you. You could have been there 400 years. Say this with me, "Lord let me meet the right people that can release Suddenlies in my life." Stop hanging around people who are not anointed, stop hanging around religious people because you will never receive a suddenly. You will find yourself doing the same thing 10 years from now. Having the same type service, being the same pastor's helper, carrying the same brief case, carrying the same cup of water you've been carrying for the last 10 years. The key to your success is going to be to get around some people who have the power of God in their mouth and when they speak, all of a sudden, something suddenly breaks in your life, your ministry goes to another level Suddenly! Tell somebody, "God is about to connect you with some anointed people and some Suddenlies are going to happen in your life." Not only that, God is going to use many of you in this room to bring some Suddenlies in somebody else's life because the anointing of God is on your life to release a suddenly. You will connect with people, who have not seen anything happen for them in years and when you prophecy, when you pray, when you preach something is about to be released in their life. It's going to be a suddenly! Somebody shout Suddenly! My assignment tonight is to tell you how to get some Suddenlies in your life. Come on, some of you need some Suddenlies, you've been stuck too long. You've been in the same place far too long and brother it's time for something to happen quickly for you. You don't have 50 more years, you don't have 30 more years, you don't have 30 more years, you're getting older, you don't have many more years. You need a sudden release. You need to come out of religion suddenly. You need a breakthrough suddenly. I'm trying to tell you how to get some Suddenlies in your life. Somebody shout suddenly!

Suddenly can come in the form of Judgment

Here is another suddenly I want to talk about. When I studied Suddenlies in Scripture, sometimes it refers to judgment. Judgment can fall suddenly. In Sodom and Gomora, judgment fell suddenly. Paul is preaching on the Island of Cypress and there is a false prophet, a Jew, by the name of Bar Jesus. Did you know there was more than one Jesus in the Bible? This is Bar Jesus he is trying to turn away the deputy from the faith and Paul turns around and says, "Blindness is coming on you." And the Scripture says immediately, a miss and a darkness came on him. Judgment came, and someone had to walk him around. Herod, is up speaking and the people said it's the voice of a god and the Bible said because Herod did not give glory unto God an angel immediately smote him, and he was eaten up with worms. Suddenlies can come on enemies when God judges His enemies suddenly. This is why sometimes people think they are getting away with stuff, because it doesn't happen for a long time and then suddenly God releases His judgment and wipes you out. It happens quickly.

Suddenly your enemies and doubts will be confounded by your success

Then the Lord told me this. He said son, tell my people, "All the people who thought that they would never be anything, never do anything, or never go anywhere, they will see them suddenly be raised up and they will suddenly be ashamed." I'm going to make your enemies suddenly ashamed. They will suddenly be in wonder, they will suddenly wonder what happened. It will happen so quick that they will not be ready for it. That's what I love about God. When God raises a man up He raises them up suddenly and all your enemies and all your haters, all of a sudden, they wonder what happened. They begin to say, "This happened too quickly" How could it happen this quick? God is a God of Suddenly! You can be last today and be first tomorrow. You can be in prison today and in the palace tomorrow. You can be feeding the sheep one day, anointed the next day, slaying Goliath the next day. God can do something so suddenly and I think God likes to do this because He likes to surprise your enemies. Tell somebody, "God is about to surprise your enemies!" He is about to surprise your haters. Come on people of God. God is about to do something so suddenly in your life that they will remember you were over here and all of a sudden, they will see you over there. They will remember you down in one place and all of a sudden you are up here. They will ask, "How did you get up here all of a sudden?" They will remember you sitting in the back and all of a sudden, they will ask, "How did you get up here" They will remember that you were sitting back crying and weeping and all of a sudden, they will ask, "How did you get on the platform?" God is about to release a suddenly, that will surprise your enemies. I like those Suddenlies. Cause your enemies say what happened? It happened so quickly, it happened so fast. God is a God of surprises. God loves to surprise people, God loves to surprise His enemies. God loves to surprise His children, God loves to do a suddenly in the lives of His people. He is a suddenly kind of God.

Prophetic Release

The Lord said, "Tell my people to begin to use their faith for some Suddenlies." Tell my people to pray for some Suddenlies. He said tell my people, to praise me for some Suddenlies. He said tell my people to get around the right anointing for some Suddenlies. He said if my people get in position, they are about to get some Suddenlies. Some sudden breakthroughs, some sudden miracles, some sudden healings, some sudden finances, some sudden visibility, some Suddenlies are about to hit your life. God is about to do more in a short period of time than you experienced in years of your life. God is going to do something in the next year that's going to supersede the first 30 years of your life. God is about to release a suddenly in your life that will take you from zero to one hundred in no time. Tell somebody to get ready for the Suddenlies. Suddenly, straightway, immediately, say it with me, "I need some immediatelies in my life." Say, "I've been waiting a long time" "I've been serving God a long time" I've been praising God a long time. I'm getting ready for some immediatelies. I receive the word of the Lord. Get ready for immediatelies. I prophecy immediatelies into your life, I prophecy Suddenlies in your life. I prophecy straightways into your life. I prophecy some Suddenlies in your finances, I prophecy some Suddenlies in your business, I prophecy some Suddenlies in your ministry, I prophecy some Suddenlies in your marriage, I prophecy some Suddenlies with your children, I prophecy sudden contracts to come into your hands, I prophecy sudden land and property to come into your hands, I prophecy sudden doors shall open, I prophecy some sudden platforms you're going to stand on. I prophecy some Suddenlies in your life in the name of Jesus. Lift your hands and receive the Suddenlies of God. I prophecy some sudden doors that were closed are going to open suddenly. I prophecy some suddenly things in your life. Suddenly blessings, suddenly breakthroughs, suddenly anointings, Suddenlies are coming to the church, suddenly we will see churches spring up, sudden growth in your church and in your ministry. I prophecy some sudden healings about to hit your body, stuff that's been bothering you for years, God is about to drive cancer out of your body suddenly, He is about to drive diabetes and high blood pressure out of your body suddenly. He is about to drive some devils that have tormented you for years, He's about to drive then out suddenly. Get ready for some suddenly deliverances. Begin to give God praise and shout hallelujah, hallelujah, hallelujah, suddenly, suddenly, suddenly. Oh yes, begin to praise God for your suddenly, praise Him for your suddenly, praise Him for your suddenly, praise Him for your suddenly! Stuff you've been waiting on for years. Stuff you've been believing God for years to come to pass, will come suddenly, promises you've been standing on for years, will come suddenly, your children will get saved suddenly. Come on and believe God that Suddenlies are coming to the church. God is about to release some surprises in your life. I prophecy surprises, surprises, surprises, surprises, from heaven, surprises. God is about to surprise you with some stuff you didn't even think about. Stuff you didn't even ask for, He's about to give you stuff you never asked for. He's going to surprise you with some new things. Somebody lift your hands and lift your voices and shout hallelujah in this place. Oh yes, I prophecy surprises, surprises, surprises from heaven, surprises, surprise us Lord. Come on and say, "Surprise me Lord, Surprise me Lord, SURPRISE ME LORD!" Don't stop praising Him, it will be praise that will release the suddenly in your life. Praise is about to release the Suddenlies in your life. Praise is about to release the Suddenlies in your life. Come on and give Him praise. Give him praise, Give Him praise, Yes Give Him praise! How many need sudden finances? I prophecy sudden finances into your life now. Sudden business, sudden contracts, Suddenlies are coming to your finances in the name of Jesus. It's going to happen suddenly because you've been giving! You've been giving, you've been sowing, so get ready for a sudden harvest. A sudden harvest is coming to your life! Listen, I heard the man of God say this and I'm going to prophecy this over you tonight. This will be the lowest place you will ever be in your life. I repeat this is the lowest place you will ever be in your life. God is about to take you higher suddenly. This will be the lowest place you will ever experience, tonight will be the lowest place because God is about to promote you suddenly! You're going up! You're going up! Get ready for your Suddenly!

Chapter 1

Suddenly God Is Doing a New Thing

See, I will do a new thing, now it shall spring forth; shall you not be aware of it? I will even make a way in the wilderness, and rivers in the desert.

                              Isaiah 43:19 (MEV)

IN ISAIAH 43:19, the prophet Isaiah is writing during a period in biblical history where God was declaring that He would do a new thing for Israel. When the prophet uses the word new, he is not only saying that it will be something never done before. In order to gain a proper understanding, it would be necessary for us to look at the Hebrew word "new" used in this instance. The word new according to Brown Driver Briggs Lexicon of Hebrew words when translated would be *chadash*, which literally means new thing but it also has a secondary meaning of fresh. Therefore, God is saying I am going to do something fresh in your life.

There are times in our lives when life has taken a toll on us and we need God to do something new. This was the underlying tone of the text. God was about to do something fresh in their lives. Have you ever needed God to do something fresh? Do you know how it feels to need Him to do it Suddenly? This was the situation the Children of Israel were in. When we research the history of the text, we find that that Israel was in a dry place spiritually, which means they were devoid of the presence of God and devoid of the saturation of the dew of His spirit. When we are dry in our spirits, we need God to do something fresh and we need Him to do it Suddenly.

Let's look at a time in the history of Israel when they needed God to do something new and fresh in their life. For this, we will look at Ezekiel 37:1-14. In this text, the prophet Ezekiel is dealing with a prophetic word he received from the Lord concerning Israel being renewed and refreshed.

Let's take a look at the text.

The Valley of Dry Bones

The hand of the Lord was upon me, and He carried me out in the Spirit of the Lord and set me down in the midst of the valley which was full of bones, and He caused me to pass among them all around. And there were very many in the open valley. And they were very dry. He said to me, "Son of man, can these bones live?" And I answered, "O Lord God, You know." Again He said to me,

2

*"Prophesy over these bones and say to them,
O dry bones, hear the word of the Lord.*

*Thus says the Lord God to these bones, "I
will cause breath to enter you so that you
live. And I will lay sinews upon you and will
grow back flesh upon you and cover you
with skin and put breath in you so that you
live. Then you shall know that I am the
Lord." So I prophesied as I was commanded.
And as I prophesied, there was a noise and
a shaking. And the bones came together,
bone to its bone. When I looked, the sinews
and the flesh grew upon them, and the skin
covered them. But there was no breath in
them. Then He said to me, "Prophesy to the
wind; prophesy, son of man, and say to the
wind. Thus, says the Lord God, come from
the four winds, O breath, and breathe upon
these slain so that they live." So I prophesied
as He commanded me, and the breath came
into them, and they lived and stood up upon
their feet, an exceeding great army.*

*Then He said to me, "Son of man, these
bones are the whole house of Israel. They
say, "Our bones are dried up, and our hope
is lost. We are cut off completely." Therefore
prophesy and say to them, thus says the*

Lord God, "Pay attention, O My people, I will open your graves and cause you to come up out of your graves and bring you into the land of Israel. Then you shall know that I am the Lord, when I have opened your graves, O My people, and brought you up out of your graves. And I shall put My Spirit in you, and you shall live, and I shall place you in your own land. Then you shall know that I the Lord have spoken and performed it, says the Lord."

Ezekiel 37:1-14 (MEV)

The Lord basically told them that He was getting ready to refresh, restore, and renew them. Just as he did it for them, he will do it for you. Suddenly is about to overtake you and cause you to be refreshed and restored! It's your Suddenly Season!

As we were praying and seeking the Lord, He gave us 30 areas where you will encounter Suddenlies in your life. This list is by no means a complete list, as you may add to it other areas where you have experienced or are expecting God to do something Suddenly for you.

Suddenly Souls coming into the Kingdom.

Suddenly You will receive Favor.

Suddenly Increase will come.

Suddenly Healing will come.

Suddenly Deliverance will come.

Suddenly Wisdom will come.

Suddenly Resources will come.

Suddenly Vision will be renewed.

Suddenly Expansion will come.

Suddenly Breakthrough will come.

Suddenly Creativity will come.

Suddenly Divine Connections will come.

Suddenly Restoration will come.

Suddenly You will have the Strength of the Ox.

Suddenly Release will come for things, which were held up.

Suddenly Acceleration will come

Suddenly Overflow will come.

Suddenly Exposure will come.

Suddenly Power will come.

Suddenly Fulfillment will come.

Suddenly Manifestation will come.

Suddenly the Fire of God will come.

Suddenly Finances will come.

Suddenly Divine Reversal will come.

Suddenly Resuscitation will come.

Suddenly Recompense will come.

Suddenly Retroactive Restitution will come.

Suddenly Boldness will come.

Suddenly Fearlessness will come.

Suddenly God will Remember You.

Get ready for God to do a new thing in your life Suddenly!

Chapter 2

The God of the Suddenly Is Coming to Your House Today

WHAT WOULD IT be like to have God show up at your house, to have access to Him in human form. A man by the name of Jairus experienced this one day as his daughter was lying on her deathbed. He realized that the only person capable of restoring the life of his daughter was Jesus. I am certain he had seen others who claimed to have been healed miraculously by one touch of the Master. Now all of a sudden, his daughter laying at the point of death and he knew that it would be worth the effort to go and find Jesus. The one who could raise the dead, heal the sick, open blind eyes, and unmute deaf ears.

However, sandwiched in the middle of this story is another story. From a Hermeneutic perspective, when this occurs it is called an Intercalation (the insertion of one story into another). While Jesus is in route to go to Jairus's house, He is touched by a woman who desperately needed an encounter with the Master. The story of the woman with the "Issue of Blood." When thinking of our topic Suddenly, it causes us to look at this story differently. Two Gospel writers tell this story and they each have different versions. Let's look at the story in Matthew 9:18-26 and Mark 5:21-43.

The Ruler's Daughter and a Woman Healed

While He was speaking these things to them, a certain ruler came and worshipped Him, saying, "My daughter is even now dead. But come and lay Your hand on her, and she will live." Jesus rose and followed him, and so did His disciples **Then a woman, who was ill with a flow of blood for twelve years, came behind Him and touched the hem of His garment. For she said within herself, "If I may just touch His garment, I shall be healed." But Jesus turned around, and when He saw her, He said, "Daughter, be of good comfort. Your faith has made you well." And the woman was made well instantly.** *When Jesus came to the ruler's house and saw the musicians and the mourners making a noise, He said to them, "Depart. The girl is not dead, but is sleeping." And they laughed Him to scorn. But when the people were put outside, He went in and took her by the hand, and the girl arose. The news of this went out into all that land.*

Matthew 9:18-26 (MEV)

Mark's Gospel Parallel to the story.

Jairus' Daughter and the Woman Who Touched Jesus' Garment

When Jesus had crossed again by boat to the other side, many people gathered to Him. And He was beside the sea. One of the rulers of the synagogue, named Jairus, saw Jesus and came and fell at His feet and earnestly asked Him, "My little daughter is lying at the point of death. I ask You, come and lay Your hands on her, so that she may be healed. And she will live." So Jesus went with him. And many people followed Him and pressed in on Him. **And a certain woman had a hemorrhage for twelve years, and had suffered much under many physicians. And had spent all that she had, and was nothing better but rather grew worse. When she had heard of Jesus, came in the crowd behind Him and touched his garment. For she said, "If I may touch but His garment, I shall be healed." And immediately, her hemorrhage dried up and she felt in her body that she was healed of the affliction. At once, Jesus knew within Himself that power had gone out of Him. He turned around in the crowd and said, "Who touched My garments?"**

His disciples said to him, "You see the crowd pressing against You, and You say, "Who touched Me?" And He looked round about to see her who had done it. But the woman, fearing and trembling, knowing what had happened to her, came and fell down before Him and told Him the entire truth.

He said to her, "Daughter, your faith has made you well. Go in peace and be whole of your affliction." *While He was still speaking, some came from the house of the synagogue ruler and said, "Your daughter is dead. Why trouble the Teacher any further?" As soon as Jesus heard the word that was spoken, He said to the ruler of the synagogue, "Do not be afraid, only believe."*

He let no one follow Him, except Peter, and James, and John the brother of James. He came to the house of the ruler of the synagogue, and saw the tumult, and those who wept and wailed loudly. When He came in, He said to them, "Why make this uproar and weep? The girl is not dead, but sleeping." They laughed at Him in ridicule. But when He had put them all out, He took the father and the mother of the girl and those who were with Him and entered where the girl was lying. He took the girl by the hand and said to her, "Talitha cumi," which means, "Little girl, I say to you, arise." Immediately the girl arose and walked, for she was twelve years of age. And they were greatly astonished. He strictly ordered them to let no one know of it and directed them to give her something to eat.

Mark 5:21-43 (MEV)

Let's take notice of several things, which the text reveals to us about both situations. First, we will look at the story of the woman with the issue of blood. In order to gain a proper perspective of the situation, we must observe the cultural and societal norms. Leviticus gives us more information concerning societal expectations of conduct within the Jewish culture for a woman who was experiencing this type issue.

And if a woman have an issue, and her issue in her flesh be blood, she shall be put apart seven days: and whosoever toucheth her, shall be unclean until the even. And everything that she lieth upon in her separation shall be unclean: everything also that she sitteth upon shall be unclean. And whosoever toucheth her bed shall wash his clothes, and bathe himself in water, and be unclean until the even. And whosoever toucheth any thing that she sat upon shall wash his clothes, and bathe himself in water, and be unclean until the even. And if it be on her bed, or on any thing whereon she sitteth, when he toucheth it, he shall be unclean until the even. And if any man lie with her at all, and her flowers be upon him, he shall be unclean seven days; and all the bed whereon he lieth shall be unclean. And if a woman have an issue of her blood many days out of the time of her separation, or if it run beyond the time of her separation; all the days of the issue of her uncleanness shall be as the days of her separation: she shall be unclean. Every bed whereon she lieth all the days of her issue shall be unto her as the bed of her separation and whatsoever she sitteth upon shall be unclean, as the uncleanness of her separation. And whosoever toucheth those things shall be unclean, and shall wash his clothes, and bathe himself in water, and be unclean until the even. But if she be cleansed of her issue, then she shall number to herself seven days, and after that she shall be clean. And on the eighth day she shall take unto her two turtles, or two young pigeons, and bring them unto the priest, to the door of the tabernacle of the congregation. And the priest shall offer the one for a sin offering, and the other for a burnt offering; and the priest shall make an atonement for her before the Lord for the issue of her uncleanness.

Leviticus 15:19-30 (KJV)

After reading this text, we understand that it was culturally and ceremonially unacceptable for her to have been in close proximity of other people. This tells us that she was in desperate need and that she was willing to violate the rules of society in order to get the healing that she needed. The first thing we establish as a prerequisite for Suddenly is need. Some may call it desperation.

As we travel to countries outside the United States and conduct missions and leadership training, occasionally, we travel to countries where people are less fortunate, economically, than people in the United States. Many times, it is said that citizens of the United States are very fortunate in many areas. One area, in particular, is in our healthcare system. Friends in other countries have stated that, it is easier for God to perform miracles in their country because they have no other alternative. They often do not have the means to afford the same level of medical care; therefore, they fully rely on God to heal them or deliver them from various ailments.

This is the situation that the woman in the story found herself in for over 12 years. She was desperate, destitute, and in need of serious help. This, in itself, would have been enough to motivate her to violate the Jewish law and cultural norms, which forbid her from being in public places and especially touching a man in public. After spending money on doctors for 12 years, the text says that instead of getting better, she was getting worse. A hemorrhage of 12 years caused her to be weak and not have her full strength on a consistent basis. She was by Jewish law required to stay away from others and when she entered into their environment she would have had to yell "unclean." It would have been difficult for her to acquire funds if she were unable to interact with others, perform work, or secure a source of employment. In Matthew's account, she was healed instantly. In Mark, the Scripture declares that she was healed immediately. Either way, suddenly from one touch she was made whole. She went from being rejected, secluded, isolated, and ostracized to being accepted and walking in good health.

All we need is one touch from the Master and all our ailments will be eradicated. The text said that she knew if she could only touch the hem of His garment, she knew she would be made whole.

The Word of God declares that God is not a respecter of persons. Therefore, whatever He does for one person, He will do for another. If He released healing *Suddenly* for the woman with the issue of blood, God will release healing *Suddenly* for you too. Scripture declares He is not a respecter of persons, so expect Him to heal you suddenly. Perhaps you don't need a physical, emotional, or relational healing. Whatever area of your life you desire for God to heal you in, you can rest assured that you will receive it, if you only believe.

Return to the story of Jairus' Daughter

The first thing we notice is that he is a ruler of the synagogue and in both texts, he is called by name. This does not always happen in Scripture but when it does, it should cause us to take notice. His position and status in the Jewish community should cause us to take a very different look at the story. Someone with the political and social status of a ruler in the synagogue would not be known to come and throw themselves down at the feet of Jesus in the open to ask for assistance. The Scripture shows us that despite his political and financial position of power, he was desperate and willing to lay aside all of it, because he needed God to perform a miracle.

Situations in life will cause us to humble ourselves and ask for help. They will also help us to understand that we need God to resurrect the dead areas in our lives. It could be children, finances, business, ministry, or marriage. No matter which area pertains to you personally, trials will cause you to submit, cry out, and worship God, who is able to do anything but fail.

Trials, tribulation, and trouble have a very special way of bringing us to a place where we lay everything aside and recognize that neither our education, good looks, connections, or ability to "smooth talk" can get us the results we need. We recognize we need Jesus to come to our house and bring resurrection. In Jairus case, it was for his daughter; but for you, there could possibly be other areas, which you need God to resurrect. Something that appears to be dead. Just as healing was released for his daughter, so will it be for your situation.

As they arrived at the house, one of the people approached Jairus and said, "Don't bother the Master, the damsel is already dead." The Scripture says that Jesus proceeds to the house.

Once Jesus arrives, He does something which is wise for all intercessors. He put everyone out of the room who were not believing in one accord for the girl's healing.

When we pray and believe God for our prayers to be answered, the last thing we need in the room are people filled with doubt.

It is important to surround yourself with like-minded people who will support your spiritual goals and growth. The only people Jesus allowed in the room were the girl's mother and father along with Peter, James, and John because they had a vested interest in seeing her become healed.

One encounter with Jesus can Suddenly change your entire life. Jesus speaks to the young lady and the Scripture declares that immediately she arises and walks. When the God of the Suddenlies arrives at your house, everything tends to change.

The text tells us that there were people who literally laughed at Jesus before he healed the young lady. Success will cause your enemies to be ashamed and astonished at what God is about to do in your life. The God of the Suddenly is coming to your house today and while He is there, He will cause dead things to rise. He will cause your enemies to be ashamed. He will cause your faith to arise. Get ready for the God of the Suddenlies to come to your house today!

Chapter 3

Suddenly The Finisher's Anointing Is Coming Upon You

I have fought a good fight, I have finished my course, I have kept the faith.

2 Timothy 4:7

PAUL THE APOSTLE was perhaps one of the most noted biblical characters of the New Testament. He is credited with having written twelve of the 27 New Testament Books. He could not have completed his assignment without the anointing to finish what he started.

In Second Timothy 4:7, he concludes an exhortation to his spiritual son Timothy with the words, "I have fought a good fight, I have finished my course, I have kept the faith." The verses prior to this, give us a clue toward understanding the message he is trying to convey.

I charge thee therefore before God, and the Lord Jesus Christ, who shall judge the quick and the dead at His appearing and His kingdom. Preach the word. Be instant in season, out of season. Reprove, rebuke, exhort with all long suffering and doctrine.

For the time will come when they will not endure sound doctrine; but after their own lusts shall they heap to themselves teachers, having itching ears; and they shall turn away their ears from the truth, and shall be turned unto fables. But watch thou in all things, endure afflictions, do the work of an evangelist, make full proof of thy ministry. For I am now ready to be offered, and the time of my departure is at hand. I have fought a good fight, I have finished my course, I have kept the faith. Henceforth, there is laid up for me a crown of righteousness, which the Lord, the righteous judge, shall give me at that day and not to me only, but unto all them also that love his appearing.

2 Timothy 4:1-8

Notice that Paul instructs Timothy to continue to do the work he was doing with all longsuffering in verse 3. He goes further in verse 5 to say that he must endure afflictions. He concludes in verse 7 with "I have fought a good fight and finished my course." When we think about this and look at his process, let us consider what Paul could have experienced, that qualified him to make such statements. There are several texts that help us gain a deeper perspective into the life, which Paul lived that qualified him to make such a statement. If Paul lived in 2017, he would be able to say, "check my resume."

One of the texts which gives us a glimpse of Paul's resume is Second Corinthians 11:23-28.

> *Are they ministers of Christ? (I speak as a fool) I am more in labours more abundant, in stripes above measure, in prisons more frequent, in deaths oft. Of the Jews five times received I forty stripes save one. Thrice was I beaten with rods, once was I stoned, thrice I suffered shipwreck, a night and a day I have been in the deep. in journeyings often, in perils of waters, in perils of robbers, in perils by mine own countrymen, in perils by the heathen, in perils in the city, in perils in the wilderness, in perils in the sea, in perils among false brethren. In weariness and painfulness, in watchings often, in hunger and thirst, in fastings often, in cold and nakedness. Beside those things that are without, that which cometh upon me daily, the care of all the churches.*
>
> *2 Corinthians 11:23-28*

Paul's experiences in ministry would mirror many of the challenges we face in ministry in today's church. However, it would be difficult to complain or to get tired if we had to compare our experiences with those which he experienced. We only get a glimpse of his "highlight reel," but the day-to-day operations of his work, we may never really comprehend. He shares many of the challenges from his three missionary journeys and his trip to Rome in Acts 13–28. It was Paul's experiences in ministry, which produced in him the Finisher's Anointing.

It is often amazing that people want to experience the same level of success as someone else, but the question we must ask ourselves is do we want to endure their process.

Paul's process gave him the experience needed to encourage others to finish strong and so will be yours.

> *For which cause we faint not, but though our outward man perish, yet the inward man is renewed day-by-day. For our light affliction, which is but for a moment, worketh for us a far more exceeding and eternal weight of glory. While we look not at the things which are seen, but at the things which are not seen, for the things which are seen are temporal, but the things which are not seen are eternal.*
>
> *2 Corinthians 4:16-18*

He is telling them that although their outward man is perishing, it's working for them. There will be many circumstances in life, which may not feel or look pleasant but it's working for your good. In life, we may be experiencing challenges but we must take a positive outlook because we realize, it could always be worse. There is always someone who would easily trade places with us. So, we need to determine that we will finish strong. We will not allow our circumstances or situations to cause us to backup, retreat, quit, or throw in the towel. We need to remind ourselves, "I am anointed to finish what I started, I have the Finisher's Anointing!"

Like apostle Paul, there will be heartaches and disappointments, there will also be challenging days but through it all, remain steadfast, unmovable, always abounding in the work of the Lord, for as much as you know, your labor is not in vain with the Lord (1 Cor. 15:58). You can rest assured that God is faithful to remember your labor of love, in that you have ministered to the saints and continue to do so. You must also know that in due season, you will reap if you faint not. You need to be like apostle Paul and be committed to complete what you start. We call this the Finisher's Anointing. The ability to persevere through the storms and trials of life, with a testimony that says, "I don't look like what I've been through" is what the Finisher's Anointing is all about.

No matter what comes your way, remember that your purpose and destiny are connected to more people than just yourself. Someone else's destiny is tied to yours and someone is watching what you are doing and patterning their life after you. If the apostle Paul had not finished his assignment, what example would Timothy and Titus have had? If Jesus had gotten off the cross at Calvary, where would we all be? It will be painful at times but we must continue and we must persevere with tenacity until our assignment is complete. I want to close with the story of a young man from Africa in the 1968 Olympics in Mexico. The story goes like this.

> "While competing in the marathon in the 1968 Olympics in Mexico City, John Stephen Akhwari cramped up due to the high altitude of the city. He had not trained at such an altitude back in his country. At the 19-kilometer point, during the 42-km race, there was jockeying for position between some runners and he was hit. He fell badly, wounding his knee and dislocating that joint; his shoulder also hit hard against the pavement. However, he continued running, finishing last among the 57 competitors who completed the race of the 75 who had begun the race. The winner of the marathon, Mamo Wolde of Ethiopia, finished in 2:20:26. Akhwari

finished in 3:25:27, when there were only a few thousand people left in the stadium, and the sun had set. A television crew was sent out from the medal ceremony when word was received that there was one more runner about to finish.

As he finally crossed the finish line, a cheer came from the small crowd. When interviewed later and asked why he continued running, he said, "My country did not send me 5,000 miles to start the race; they sent me 5,000 miles to finish the race!"

The Finisher's Anointing wasn't just for him nor is it just for a select group of people, it also applies to you. We have seen over the last few years, God suddenly release the Finisher's Anointing upon numerous people who had seemingly given up. One young man in particular who was one of the attendees and graduates of our Discipleship Training Institute had given up for 20 years on completing his bachelor's degree. There was that one class which appeared to be too difficult for him to pass. Once he began to make the decrees and declarations contained in this book, he contacted the school and as a result in our 2017 Discipleship Training Institute graduation he received not only his Discipleship Diploma but also his diploma from the college he had attended. That's right, he finished his degree. With tears in his eyes he accepted the degree he had been wanting for years but had given up on.

Another young lady who had been following the suddenly prayers at midnight and teachings on Facebook and YouTube got the courage to return to school also and as a result she completed her degree as well. You too can complete what you've started. Maybe it was a business, a family, a book, or even a ministry. Life comes at us all and often times our only recourse is to give up, to stop running our race but we are decreeing that you will go back and finish whatever it is that you started and this time you will not stop until you complete it.

Our declaration is that the Finisher's Anointing is coming upon us now so that we can finish every assignment, which we have been given. We did not start the race only to quit a portion on the way through. We started the race to finish and finish strong is what we will do. You will not quit, you will not give up and you will not give in, but you will finish. You will complete your assignments in the earth with the utmost excellence and power. Receive the Finisher's Anointing Suddenly!

Chapter 4

Suddenly You Shall Pursue, Overtake, and Recover All

And David enquired of the Lord, saying, "Shall I pursue after this troop? Shall I overtake them?" And He answered him, "Pursue, for thou shalt surely overtake them, and without fail recover all."

1 Samuel 30:8 (KJV)

HAVE YOU EVER lost something that really meant a lot to you? Maybe it was a family heirloom passed down for many years through your family line. That would be a tragedy; however, it would be even worse if it had been stolen from you. The feeling alone of having someone steal something makes you feel violated. In the midst of feeling hurt, confused, and sad about what you lost, you simultaneously begin to become angry.

This is the situation David found himself in when he returned home in First Samuel 30. He had come back home only to find out that an opposing group of soldiers had come and invaded his encampment and taken away his family and possessions.

And it came to pass, when David and his men came to Ziklag on the third day, that the Amalekites had invaded the south and smitten Ziklag, and burned it with fire. And had taken the women captives, that were therein, they slew not any, either great or small, but carried them away, and went on their way. So David and his men came to the city, and, behold, it was burned with fire; and their wives, and their sons, and their daughters, were taken captives. Then David and the people that were with him lifted up their voice and wept, until they had no more power to weep. And David's two wives were taken captives, Ahinoam the Jezreelitess, and Abigail the wife of Nabal the Carmelite. And David was greatly distressed, for the people spake of stoning him, because the soul of all the people was grieved, every man for his sons and for his daughters, but David encouraged himself in the Lord his God.

1 Samuel 30:1-6 (KJV)

The text says that the enemy had come in and taken their possessions and burned their encampment. This meant that they had lost everything. Deep down, the feeling of loss and despair will produce a multitude of emotions. Verse

3 says that David and the men who were with him wept until they had no more power to weep. Along with anger comes a feeling of despair, which stems from the fact that you really have no clue what to do. At this point, because of the relationship David had with God, the story tells us that David first encourages himself in the Lord. Once he is encouraged, he then enquires as to whether it is the Lord's will for him to pursue the enemy. Many of us would not have been like David, most of us would have immediately pursued the enemy. We would ask God for permission later, but David had learned that it is impossible to fight against the will of God. When David enquires, the Lord answers and says, "Surely you shall pursue, overtake and recover all."

Many who read this book have encountered circumstances, where the enemy has stolen something from you. Whether it be in your marriage, your finances, your ministry, your self-esteem, or even your voice or your strength. Whatever the enemy has come in and taken, you want it back. Not only do you want it back, you want it back now. We're sure this was how David felt. He wanted that which belonged to him and he wanted it yesterday.

Here is the interesting twist to the story. The enemy who had stolen from David was also an enemy to Israel and God. Anytime someone or something is an enemy to God, it's in trouble. So, when David enquired of the Lord, he received an emphatic yes! You shall pursue, overtake, and recover all.

One of the things we have learned is that whichever enemy you leave alive in this generation, it will eventually affect your descendants in the next generations. Some shortcomings may appear to be small or insignificant but if left alive, they have the capability to multiply and become dangerous.

This was the case with the Amalekites. We initially hear about the Amalekites in the Book of Genesis where Moses and the Children of Israel are leaving Egypt. The Amalekites were descendants of Esau, the brother of Jacob, and although they were distant cousins to Israel, they attacked them as they were leaving Egypt.

The next encounter Israel has with them is when Moses is upon the mountain and Aaron and Hur hold his arms up, while Joshua is fighting with them in the valley.

> *Then came Amalek, and fought with Israel in Rephidim. And Moses said unto Joshua, "Choose us out men, and go out, fight with Amalek tomorrow, I will stand on the top of the hill with the rod of God in mine hand." So Joshua did as Moses had said to him, and fought with Amalek. and Moses, Aaron, and Hur went up to the top of the hill. And it came*

to pass, when Moses held up his hand, that Israel prevailed, and when he let down his hand, Amalek prevailed. But Moses hands were heavy, and they took a stone, and put it under him, and he sat thereon; and Aaron and Hur lifted up his hands, the one on the one side, and the other on the other side; and his hands were steady until the going down of the sun. And Joshua discomfited Amalek and his people with the edge of the sword.

Exodus 17:8-13

It was here that God makes a declaration that He would have war with Amalek from year to year. This would also be the place where we first hear of God referred to as Jehovah Nissi (The Lord is our banner). Which correlates with the text of Isaiah 59:18-19, which says that when the enemy comes in like a flood, the Lord will lift up a standard (banner or flag) against him.

And Moses built an altar, and called the name of it Jehovah Nissi (that is, The Lord our banner); for he said, "Because the Lord hath sworn that the Lord will have war with Amalek from generation to generation."

Exodus 17:15-16 (CKJ - KJ21)

According to their deeds, accordingly he will repay, fury to his adversaries, recompense to his enemies; to the islands he will repay

*recompense. So shall they fear the name of the
Lord from the west, and His glory from the
rising of the sun. When the enemy shall come
in like a flood, the Spirit of the Lord shall lift
up a standard against him.*

Isaiah 59:18-19

To someone who has never been either in or
around the military, this would not make much
sense; however, for someone who has an
understanding of the military, we know that every
military unit has a guidon (flag or banner) and
when they are in battle, the commander carries that
guidon. When the battle gets hot, we rally around
the flag and we fight for the flag, banner, or guidon.
It is a symbol of pride for a soldier. Likewise, God is
Who we, as Christian soldiers, rally around when
the enemy attacks us. When your enemy surrounds
you, whoever or whatever it may be, look to God as
your Strong Tower. Scripture tells us that we can
run to Him and be safe. He is our victory, He is our
strength, and it is to Him that we look when we face
the toughest battles of our lives. He and He alone
can deliver us and bring us out unharmed.

Fast-forward a few hundred years, and King
Saul is given an instruction from the prophet
Samuel to destroy the Amalekites. The problem is
that for some reason he leaned to his own
understanding and did not obey what the Lord

instructed him to do in its entirety. Remember, partial obedience is total disobedience.

Samuel's Instruction from the Lord

One day, Samuel told Saul, "the Lord had me choose you to be king of his people, Israel. Now listen to this message from the Lord," "When the Israelites were on their way out of Egypt, the nation of Amalek attacked them. I am the Lord All-Powerful, and now I am going to make Amalek pay! Go and attack the Amalekites! Destroy them and all their possessions. Don't have any pity. Kill their men, women, children, and even their babies. Slaughter their cattle, sheep, camels, and donkeys."

1 Samuel 15:1-3 (CEV)

Saul's Disobedience

And Saul smote the Amalekites from Havilah until thou comest to Shur, that is over against Egypt. And he took Agag, the king of the Amalekites, alive, and utterly destroyed all the people with the edge of the sword. But Saul and the people spared Agag, and the best of the sheep, and of the oxen, and of the fatlings, and the lambs, and all that was good, and would not utterly destroy them; but everything that was vile and refuse, that they destroyed utterly. Then came the word of the Lord unto Samuel, saying, "It repenteth Me that I have set up Saul to be king, for he has turned back from following Me, and hath not performed My commandments." And it grieved Samuel, and he cried unto the Lord all night.

And when Samuel rose early to meet Saul in the morning, it was told Samuel, saying, Saul came to Carmel, and, behold, he set him up a place, and is gone about, and passed on, and gone down to Gilgal. And Samuel came to Saul, and Saul said unto him, "Blessed be thou of the Lord. I have performed the commandment of the Lord." And Samuel said, "What meaneth then this bleating of the sheep in mine ears, and the lowing of the oxen which I hear?" And Saul said, "They have brought them from the Amalekites, for the people spared the best of the sheep and of the oxen, to sacrifice unto the Lord thy God and the rest we have utterly destroyed." Then Samuel said unto Saul, "Stay, and I will tell thee what the Lord hath said to me this night." And he said unto him, "Say on." And Samuel said, "When thou wast little in thine own sight, wast thou not made the head of the tribes of Israel, and the Lord anointed thee king over Israel? And the Lord sent thee on a journey, and said, "Go and utterly destroy the sinners the Amalekites, and fight against them until they be consumed."

Wherefore then didst thou not obey the voice of the Lord, but didst fly upon the spoil, and didst evil in the sight of the Lord?" And Saul said unto Samuel, "Yea, I have obeyed the voice of the Lord, and have gone the way which the Lord sent me, and have brought Agag the king of Amalek, and have utterly destroyed the Amalekites. But the people took of the spoil, sheep and oxen, the chief of the things which should have been utterly destroyed, to sacrifice unto the Lord thy God in Gilgal." And Samuel said, "Hath the Lord as great delight in burnt offerings and sacrifices, as in obeying the voice of the Lord? Behold, to obey is better than sacrifice, and to hearken than the fat of rams.

For rebellion is as the sin of witchcraft, and stubbornness is as iniquity and idolatry. Because thou hast rejected the word of the Lord, he hath also rejected thee from being king."

1 Samuel 15:7-23

One act of obedience can change your entire world; likewise, one act of disobedience can also destroy years of hard work and building. In Saul's case, his initial claim was that he did a good deed by leaving the best of things alive along with the king. The problem here is that he kept the king alive, who now had the ability to produce an offspring. Likewise, any sin or area in our lives, which we do not crucify, can come back with a vengeance. The key here is not just that your decisions affect you, but the decisions we make today tend to cause repercussions for generations to come. History has proven that our issues and problems we don't addresses are often passed down to the next generations, if we don't destroy it.

The Amalekites, which Saul left alive during his time, were the same Amalekites who came in and robbed, pillaged, and kidnapped during David's time. Had Saul been obedient during his reign as king, David would never have had to suffer distress and despair at the hand of the Amalekites.

***

We must identify unresolved areas in our lives that we have warred with, that may be left for our children, grandchildren, and great grandchildren to have to contend with. Will you allow poverty, lust, perversion, anger, fear, procrastination, poor self-image, gluttony, or greed to be the issue that attacks your loved ones in the future?

We are certain that you will make the determination as David did, that you are determined to go and pursue the enemy, destroy him, and take back everything which belongs to you. We must pursue our enemy violently. The word used for "pursue" when translated in the Hebrew is the word *radaf*, translated according to the *Brown, Driver, Briggs Hebrew-English Lexicon* means to be behind, follow after, pursue, run after, to violently chase with the intent to capture and secure. Thus, we would understand that David was given the command to chase after the enemy violently. If the enemy has attacked our family in any area, this is the type of tenacity and determination we must run after our enemy with, in order to overtake him and secure that which belongs to us. The good news is that when David overtook and recovered all, he not only recovered his family and secured enough spoil for himself, but enough for all those who were left behind and the generations to come.

This is the season for you to violently chase and destroy everything which has plagued your family for generations. First, so that it has no chance of plaguing the future generations. Second, so that you can recover everything, which he stole from you.

War always inherently brings with it spoils for those who fight and overcome. Once you overcome the enemy, you will reap the spoils that come with victory. Once you have defeated your enemy and developed a war plan for defeating it, many others who deal with the same enemy will come and sit at your feet to understand how you overcame it.

You are called to provide solutions in the earth for problems. If your family has battled with poverty, your assignment in the earth is to break the cycle of generational poverty and create generational wealth. If your battle has been against anger or fear, you will have opportunities to help others with similar challenges. Wherever your pain is, therein you will find your purpose. Don't allow your enemy to win by getting away with causing you pain. Make him pay for every tear you've cried. Make him pay for every scar and every wound you have received in battle. Make him wish he never attacked your family. It's time for you to pursue, overtake, and Suddenly recover all! Like David, you will not stop because you are tired. You will not stop because of how you feel, because you know that it's bigger than you. This enemy must die, because your heritage depends upon it. Go forth and violently pursue. You shall Suddenly and surely recover all with spoils. It's your Suddenly Season!

Chapter 5

Suddenly God Is Remembering You

And God remembered Rachel, and God hearkened to her, and opened her womb.

Genesis 30:22

DURING OUR MIDNIGHT Cry prayer and our 1:00 p.m. teachings on Facebook Live, we received so much feedback. Many people were encouraged who had previously struggled with feeling alone or forgotten. Life has a tendency to take us through storms, which leave us feeling alone and isolated. We can even feel as if though God has forgotten us. Nothing could be farther from the truth. When we look in Scripture, we find many passages where God remembers His people.

This chapter is specifically dedicated to those who feel like you have been in your situation so long and it feels like no one is there for you. Family has forsaken you, children, husbands, or wives. You have battled with depression and secretly had thoughts of ending it all. We want you to know that God has not forgotten you and He is about to remember you and turn your situation around. God is Suddenly remembering you! Just as God remembered Hannah, He will remember you. Just as He remembered Rachel, He will remember you. As He remembered His covenant with Abraham, Jacob, and Isaac, He will remember you. Get ready to flourish. Prepare to be victorious like you have never been before. It's your Suddenly Season and God is remembering you Suddenly. Let's look at how God remembered Hannah, Rachel, Noah, and Israel.

God Remembers Noah

> *And God **remembered** Noah, and every living thing, and all the cattle that was with him in the ark and God made a wind to pass over the earth, and the waters assuaged.*
>
> *Genesis 8:1*

God remembered Noah and caused all the waters, which covered the earth to be abated. Water is often prophetically symbolic for several things. For example, in this situation, water is symbolic for trouble, turbulence, and judgment. The earth had been covered with water as judgment for the sins of mankind. Noah had been in the ark according to the text for 150 days and it probably felt like he had been forgotten. The good news is that God is faithful and He promises to never leave us or forsake us. In the case of Noah, God remembered him and sent a wind to cause the waters, which covered the earth to be removed.

This is a season where God is remembering you and He is causing the challenges, storms, and trials of life to be blown away by the wind of His spirit. You have endured and you have not given up. You have pressed through and not allowed your situation to destroy you or make you quit. For some, you are barely holding on but guess what, you haven't quit. God is remembering you and He is causing all the challenges in this season to be Suddenly removed.

God Remembers Rachel

*And God **remembered** Rachel, and God hearkened to her, and opened her womb.*

Genesis 30:22

Rachel had to watch the other women in her husband's life produce children. She watched Leah produce children, as well as her own handmaid and Leah's handmaid. This had to be devastating inside her heart. Most of us could not even imagine what she experienced. More so, we would not have allowed it to happen. She was in agony in her spirit and soul. Then God, all of a sudden, straightway, without notice, and Suddenly remembers her.

Rachel's womb opens and she gives birth to a son named Joseph. Joseph becomes the son who would save his brothers and his father from famine. Joseph becomes the first and only Israelite to serve as the prime minister of Egypt. Could it be possible that the reason you have endured so much struggle and pain to birth your dream is because of what you are carrying? Could it be that what you are carrying is much bigger than what others are carrying? What is it that you are carrying? What's the seemingly impossible dream, which appears to be so difficult to birth?

God is remembering you and He is about to open your womb and you are about to give birth to a Joseph. You are about to give birth to someone who will change the trajectory of the way you and your family have known life to be. God has not forgotten you. He is remembering you.

God Remembers His Covenant

> *And it came to pass in process of time, that the king of Egypt died and the Children of Israel sighed by reason of the bondage, and they cried. And their cry came up unto God by reason of the bondage. And God heard their groaning, and God **remembered** his covenant with Abraham, with Isaac, and with Jacob. And God looked upon the Children of Israel, and God had respect unto them.*
>
> *Exodus 2:23-25*

Joseph was remembered and it produced peace for the Children of Israel for many years, until one day, the king died with whom Joseph had favor. The new King made life much harder on the Children of Israel. As a result of the bondage and unfair treatment, the Children of Israel began to cry out to God. It's interesting to note that the text does not say God remembered His covenant with Joseph; but He remembered His covenant with Abraham, Isaac, and Jacob. Some might remark that Jacob was a trickster and a surplanter. But when God makes a promise, it's a promise. When He makes a covenant, it's a covenant.

We once told a story of a young man who had gotten into trouble, but he had a praying mother. His mother prayed and reminded God of the covenant she had made with Him. God heard this mother's voice and freed her child because of the covenant she had made with Him years before. She called on God to remember His covenant with Solomon in Second Chronicles 7:14, which says, "If my people who are called by my name, will humble themselves and pray and seek my face, I will hear from heaven and heal their land." The word heal, when translated in the original Hebrew, equates to "restore favor to." This is God's response to Solomon's question if God's people had made mistakes and were driven from the land that was theirs. Solomon wanted to know if He would bring them back if they repented. God's answer was yes. I will remember my covenant with you and for your sake, I will deliver them.

Israel receives the benefit of the inheritance, which God promised to Abraham, Isaac, and Jacob. God remembers them and respects them because of the relationship He had with their forefathers. This means that if He remembered the covenant with Abraham, Isaac, and Jacob and had respect unto Israel, then He will do the same for you. His word says that He is not a respecter of persons; therefore, God is remembering His covenant with you, your ancestors; and He will remember His covenant with you, when it comes to your lineage. Get ready for God to Suddenly remember you and bring you out of every area of bondage in your life. There is nothing too hard for God and He is faithful to bring you out.

God Remembers Hannah

> *And they rose up in the early morning and worshipped before the Lord, and returned, and came to their house to Ramah, and Elkanah knew Hannah his wife. And the Lord **remembered** her. Wherefore it came to pass, when the time was come about after Hannah had conceived, that she bore a son, and called his name Samuel, saying, "Because I have asked him of the Lord."*
>
> *1 Samuel 1:19-20*

Hannah represents those like Rachel who feel barren, stagnant, and unfruitful in life. Her womb is locked up and it appears to her, just like many of the others that God is not hearing her cry for help.

Hannah's adversary was in her own home and she was mocking her. Peninah had been able to conceive and as a result, she used it as a means of taunting Hannah. Hannah must have felt abandoned and unappreciated. Although her husband attempted to comfort her, as a woman she felt as if she was not fulfilling her purpose in life. One day, she and her husband Elkanah went to the temple to worship. Her worship was so intense that she touched the heart of God and as a result, God remembered her and opened her womb.

Again, here is a barren woman who was carrying a very important package. Hannah births a young man by the name of Samuel. Samuel was the first Judge and Prophet of Israel. He was the one who ordained and consecrated the first two kings of Israel. He was the one who restored pure and true worship in Israel. He was also the one who established the first school of the prophets. Samuel was no ordinary child.

In life, the things that we wait the longest for and toil the most over are usually the things we appreciate most. You are called to do great things and just because it appears that it has taken a bit longer than anticipated to birth your promise, it does not signify that God has forgotten you. It means that what you have will be remembered long after those who provoked you have faded into history. If you notice, none of Peninah's sons are mentioned by name, nor do they do anything significant. Don't allow those who appear to be prospering ahead of you, make you anxious or cause you to want to compete or even compare your journey with theirs. It is God who sets up one and takes down another. Scripture declares that promotion comes neither from the east nor the west but it comes from God. One of our favorite Scriptures comes from Galatians 6:9, which says, "Be not weary in well doing, for in due season you shall reap if you faint not."

***

This is the season where God is about to remember you and your tears, your labor, your sacrifice, your obedience, and your faithfulness. He is about to not only remember you but He is about to open your womb and you will give birth to a peculiar child who will make a difference in the world. He will be one who does the unprecedented for Ages to come and his name will be known globally. Get ready to be remembered and get ready to birth a Samuel. God is remembering you and it will be Suddenly, so get ready!

Chapter 6
Destroying the Enemies of Your Suddenly

Anything great will have opposition. It would be naïve to think that with all the promises we have from God that you would just waltz down the lane of "receive your blessing" without a fight. The enemy of your soul will always put up a fight. This chapter is dedicated to identifying the enemies of your Suddenly season and destroying them. The enemies of your suddenly are procrastination, slothfulness, fear, sin, and doubt and unbelief.

The promises of God for this season in your life are so much bigger than you and like we discussed in the last chapter we have to be ready to pursue, overtake, and recover all. We cannot allow anything to stand in the way of the breakthrough and the life that comes with your suddenly season. Therefore, we will destroy all that opposes our Suddenly Season.

Procrastination

Procrastination is an enemy to your Suddenly Season. Procrastination is defined by Disctionary.com, as the act or habit of procrastinating or putting off or delaying things, especially something requiring immediate action. The Scriptures are emphatic about it. Here are several Scriptures, which address the topic of procrastination.

- Procrastinators always look for an excuse

If the clouds be full of rain, they empty themselves upon the earth: and if the tree fall toward the south, or toward the north, in the place where the tree falleth, there it shall be. He that observeth the wind shall not sow; and he that regardeth the clouds shall not reap.
   Ecclesiastes 11:3-4 King James Version (KJV)

- Ants are more industrious than Procrastinators

Go to the ant, thou sluggard; consider her ways, and be wise:Which having no guide, overseer, or ruler, Provideth her meat in the summer, and gathereth her food in the harvest.
   Proverbs 6:6-8 King James Version (KJV)

- Procrastinators are always empty handed

The soul of the sluggard desireth, and hath nothing: but the soul of the diligent shall be made fat.

Proverbs 13:4 King James Version (KJV)

- Procrastinators have to work for others

The hand of the diligent shall bear rule: but the slothful shall be under tribute.
Proverbs 12:24 King James Version (KJV)

- Procrastinators have to beg to Survive

The sluggard will not plow by reason of the cold; therefore shall he beg in harvest, and have nothing.
Proverbs 20:4 King James Version (KJV)

- Procrastinators become Poor

He becometh poor that dealeth with a slack hand: but the hand of the diligent maketh rich.
Proverbs 10:4 King James Version (KJV)

- Procrastinators love sleep

As a door turns on its hinges, so does a sluggard on his bed.
Proverbs 26:14

These Scriptures show us that people who procrastinate always put things off, they always have excuses and they love sleep. They will put things off for later, which should be done now. This type of behavior always leads to poverty and to beg. This is not the best that God has for His children and certainly it's not what anyone should desire for their life. Procrastination is a thief and it will steal, kill, and destroy your Suddenly Season. You deserve more than poverty. However, If you don't change some of your methods of operation, your end-state will be poverty.

Slothfulness

The next enemy of your suddenly season is slothfulness. The word slothful literally means "lazy" and unfortunately this is another enemy of your suddenly season. Productivity and success are tied to being industrious. The person who is slothful would rather just lie around all day and never achieve anything. Just as success is tied to hard work so is poverty to slothfulness. Many of the same Scriptures, which we connected to procrastination can also be attributed to slothfulness.

> *When you vow a vow to God, do not delay paying it, for he has no pleasure in fools. Pay **what you vow**. It is better that you should not vow than that you should vow and not pay.*
>
> *Ecclesiastes 5:4-5*

What we have learned in our personal life is that procrastination and slothfulness are arch enemies of your suddenly. I remember when social media began to take a turn toward more live videos. I procrastinated and as a result it causes us to be months behind where we could have been if we hadn't allowed the spirit of procrastination and slothfulness to hold us up. Don't allow the spirits of procrastination to hold you up and hinder what God wants to do in your life.

Fear

The another enemy which we will take a look at is the enemy called fear. Fear paralyses us and keeps us from actually stepping out to receive those things, which have been promised to us. I can remember many times in my life when my circumstances produced a fear, which kept me from moving into the promises of God. One of the Scriptures which always comes to mind is in Second Timothy 1:7. It declares that God has not given us the spirit of fear.

> *For God has not given us a spirit of fear, but of power and of love and of a sound mind.*
>
> *2 Timothy 1:7 New King James Version (NKJV)*

After having read this Scripture, I began to wonder who then has given the spirit of fear to the believer. Some groups would automatically give credit to the devil. Saying it's the devil who gives us fear. I don't totally agree with this thought process. I believe that fear comes from inside us and can often times even be environmental and / or generational. For instance, if a parent is afraid of spiders, animals, or snakes and when they see them they automatically run, then that same fear will be passed down to their child. Likewise, if when they see the spider, animal, or snake and the parent shows no fear and teaches the child that it poses no threat, often the child will then follow.

One day when one of our sons was very young we were in the mall and there was a small horse merry-go-round. He looked at the horse and his eyes enlarged as he began to yell with fear. He was petrified of the horse and began to run. Although his older sister had gotten on the horse with no problems, he was determined not to get on. However, when I jumped on the horse and then beckoned for him to join me he immediately stopped crying and began to join me. He realized that although it looked scary it posed no threat because I had overcome it. You see fear can be learned and it can be unlearned. The key to unlearning fear is to change the perspective in our minds, which causes us to perceive that whatever we are facing poses a threat.

The best way to change our phobias and fears is to recondition our minds concerning the Father's love for us. When we know that the Father is with us, we will not fear because we know that He will protect us. It is important for every believer to know what God says in His word about fear so that we can become fearless.

Another story which comes to mind is the story of the little boy who was walking to school. He walked past a gate and there was a dog in the yard that began to bark ferociously. Amazingly enough, the young boy turned around and ran quickly back home to get his father. The boy grabbed his father's hand and asked him to walk him past the yard where the dog was. When the father walked alongside the son, the son had no fear. We as believers must know that when we walk beside the Father, we have no fear. Do you remember the words of David in Psalm 23:4 wherein he says,

Yea, though I walk through the valley of the shadow of death, I will fear no evil: for thou art with me; thy rod and thy staff they comfort me.

Psalm 23:4 King James Version (KJV)

Here are a couple more Scriptures which you must memorize and when the enemy of your suddenly season rears his ugly head, you can began to remind him that your Father is on the horse with you or when he attempts to bark at you remind him that his threats don't scare you because your Father is walking with you.

For I the Lord thy God will hold thy right hand, saying unto thee, Fear not; I will help thee.

Isaiah 41:13 King James Version (KJV)

I sought the Lord, and he heard me, and delivered me from all my fears.

Psalm 34:4 King James Version (KJV)

The Lord is my light and my salvation; whom shall I fear? the Lord is the strength of my life; of whom shall I be afraid?

Psalm 27:1 King James Version (KJV)

For I am persuaded, that neither death, nor life, nor angels, nor principalities, nor powers, nor things present, nor things to come, Nor height, nor depth, nor any other creature, shall be able to separate us from the love of God, which is in Christ Jesus our Lord.

Romans 8:38-39 King James Version (KJV)

Remember God is not a respecter of persons. If He protected David, Isaiah, and Paul, more so, just as he has protected our family through challenges and dangers unseen. He loves you and will protect you as well. Always know that He will protect you and your future, and everything connected to it. Do not fear! Replace your (False Evidence that appears Real) with Faith (Forsaking All I Trust Him). You are protected by a loving Father, so step out and receive your suddenly season now.

Sin

Sin is an enemy of your suddenly season because it causes a separation between you and God. In Isaiah 59:1-2, the prophet Isaiah was speaking to the Children of Israel and sharing with them that it was not because God had an inability or a problem which kept Him from moving in their situation but more so, their sin had kept them from God, from moving from them.

> *Behold, the Lord's hand is not shortened, that it cannot save; neither his ear heavy, that it cannot hear:*

> *But your iniquities have separated between you and your God, and your sins have hid his face from you, that he will not hear.*

> *Isaiah 59:1-2 King James Version (KJV)*

Such is the case with our Suddenlies. It is not that God cannot do it and does not want to, but that often there is an area in our lives wherein we have violated the laws of God. If you were to do an inventory of your life and go through to see where you are not aligned with the perfect design of God for your life what would you see? I can look back at my own life and see where there were areas in which my life did not please God and as a result my sin became an enemy of my breakthrough. In the next chapter, we will discuss how repentance and spiritual cleansing can be powerful catalysts to obtaining our Suddenlies. We will also discuss how fasting can be a powerful catalyst for breakthrough to our Suddenlies.

Doubt/unbelief

The next enemy is doubt. I once read somewhere that doubt could be defined as an insult against the divine veracity. In other words, doubt is an insult against God because God is capable of anything but failing so when we doubt Him it's like a slap in the face for lack of better words. Honestly, that's a strong statement. It would seem blasphemous to say that a person, a human, can actually slap God but really that's about what it looks like when we don't believe Him.

There is a text in Mark 6: 5 and Matthew 13: 58 wherein it says, "Could not do many miracles there because of their unbelief". The text is referring to Jesus and His inability to perform miracles in a certain city because of the people's inability to believe in Him. How could it be that everywhere else people experienced miracles, healings, breakthroughs, and deliverances and now he comes to this city and all of a sudden, Jesus, the son of God, He who became flesh was now incapable of performing miracles. The people had placed handcuffs on Him and limited Him. The picture that comes to mind is that of superman when kryptonite is close, it literally paralyses superman. Doubt and unbelief will stop God from being able to produce in our lives.

Excuses

God hates excuses. Why?, because excuses are an enemy to our Suddenlies. Just like fear, procrastination, sin, doubt and unbelief, or excuses can limit God. Do you remember Moses on the mountain before God and Moses begins to give God reasons why he could not be used. Many of us have given God excuses for why He cannot do what He promised or even what we have asked for.

Have you ever been around someone with great potential but for some reason they say things like, "I'm not qualified" "I'm not good enough" "I wasn't born like this or that". In giving her testimony Valora often says, "Moses gave God 11 reasons why God couldn't use him and I topped his list of reasons why I couldn't do what God called me to do because of what I thought were insufficiencies." Isn't it interesting how in life we can gain perspectives and viewpoints about ourselves which cause us to produce excuses for why we either are not qualified to receive the promises of God or why although He may do it for someone else He probably won't do it for us. Today is the day to destroy the enemy of your suddenly called excuse.

Whenever excuse tries to rear his ugly head you will remind him that you are who God says you are. You will remind him that you are not leaning on your own strength but the strength that your Father in heaven provides. Your faith is not in yourself but in Him whom you live and breathe and have your being.

This list of enemies of your suddenly season is not extensive. These are the most common enemies, which we have over the years heard believers share. You may be able to look into your own life and make a list of the enemies of your suddenly. Once you make the list, go into the text of Scripture and find the weapon that helps you destroy the enemy that has attempted to stop your breakthrough. Meditate on the Scripture, quote the Scripture, and stand on the Scripture until you've dethroned every enemy of your suddenly and replaced it with the Word of God so much so that nothing hinders your ability to move into your destiny. Great things are ahead of you and you must have the courage to move into and possess that which belongs to you.

Chapter 7
Catalyst for Your Sudden Breakthrough

The term catalyst is defined as a substance, which becomes an agent for change. Therefore, just as there are enemies of our suddenly there are also catalyst for our suddenly season. Catalyst are things which can cause our suddenly to manifest quicker than normal. In our personal life, we have seen the powerful effects of these catalysts to produce a sudden change in our situation. Some of the catalysts we have seen which have produced acceleration are worship, unity, giving, faith, repentance, prayer, and fasting. In some cases, they can be used alone and in other cases you will see them coupled with other things which in turn produces the catalyst.

Unity

Unity can be seen throughout the Bible as a catalyst for Suddenlies. For instance, take a look at what happened in Genesis at the tower of Babel.

> *Now the whole earth had one language and one speech. And it came to pass, as they journeyed from the east, that they found a plain in the land of Shinar, and they dwelt*

there. Then they said to one another, "Come, let us make bricks and bake them thoroughly." They had brick for stone, and they had asphalt for mortar. And they said, "Come, let us build ourselves a city, and a tower whose top is in the heavens; let us make a name for ourselves, lest we be scattered abroad over the face of the whole earth." But the Lord came down to see the city and the tower which the sons of men had built. And the Lord said, "Indeed the people are one and they all have one language, and this is what they begin to do; now nothing that they propose to do will be withheld from them.

Genesis 11:1-9 New King James Version (NKJV)

In this instance, the unity of the people caused God to take notice from Heaven and come down to see what was going on. I have found in my life that when God sees our consolidated faith and our corporate unity it produces Suddenlies. Another Scripture which exemplifies this point is given in Acts 2.

When the Day of Pentecost had fully come, they were all with one accord in one place. And suddenly there came a sound from heaven, as of a rushing mighty wind, and it filled the whole house where they were sitting. Then there appeared to them divided tongues, as of fire, and one sat upon each of them. And they were all filled with the Holy Spirit and began to speak with other tongues, as the Spirit gave them utterance.

Acts 2:1-4 New King James Version (NKJV)

There is power when we become connected and really pursue things together. Whether in ministry, business, our family, or even our personal lives; if we find those with whom we can collaborate and create synergy, we will see the results will produce great rewards.

The catalyst of unity produces a synergy, which always leads to Suddenlies. I once read a story about a contest in which oxen were competing to pull the most weight. The story went like this, the winning ox was able to pull 8,000 pounds. As a result, the owners began to wonder how much two oxen could pull together. Many people made assumptions and gave their perspective on what the result would be. The consensus was around 16,000 pounds which people thought the two oxen combined would be able to pull. To their surprise, when the oxen were teamed together, they were able to pull 26,000 pounds.

This principle holds true in every area of life. When we team up with others we can see the powerful effects of working together to produce Suddenlies.

Today, be deliberate in connecting with other people to collaborate. Find people to pray with, to partner with in business, ministry, or family. Find those whose ideas cause you to get stirred and who make your spiritual baby leap. Find those with whom you can connect, who have the same interests and goals. Those who are heading in the same direction and watch how it produces a powerful suddenly in your life. We are praying for God to connect you with divine connections and intercessions that produce sudden breakthrough in your life, family, ministry, business, and every area of your life.

Praise and Worship

Our praise and worship are powerful catalysts for the Suddenlies of God. There is something that happens when we praise God that is totally unexplainable. When we look at the situation apostle Paul was in, in Acts 16: 25-26, we realize it was only the supernatural power of God which produced the suddenly. However, as we see in the text, the suddenly itself was produced by their unified prayer and praise.

And at midnight Paul and Silas prayed, and sang praises unto God: and the prisoners

heard them. And suddenly there was a great
earthquake, so that the foundations of the
prison were shaken: and immediately all the
doors were opened, and every one's bands
were loosed.

Acts 16:25-26 King James Version (KJV)

Have you ever heard that your praise is a weapon. We believe it is absolutely a weapon, which produces great results and sudden manifestations of the promises of God.

On several occasions in my life, I can see the fruit of praise and worship. I remember one time in my life when I was facing a very tough financial situation. As a matter of fact, I had a financial situation that required me to make the payment on the Monday morning. I went to church that Sunday morning and my situation looked pretty bleak. During praise and worship, I felt a release and as if though a weight had been lifted. When I left the church that day I just had a peace that God was going to do what I had been praying for. The next day when I went to deal with my situation I was told that for some reason the debt no longer existed. I actually argued with the person telling them, "No just Friday your office said that the total amount due was a certain amount." The young lady behind the counter looked at me and said, "Sir, your account is paid in full."

I can remember another time when we saw first-hand the effects of praise and worship. In September 2017, one of the worst Hurricanes to hit Florida in some time was headed our way. The reports had fluctuated several times during the days preceding the actual arrival of Hurricane Irma. One thing we knew was that it had caused devastation in the Caribbean and South Florida and it was headed our way. Many of our neighbors boarded up their homes and prepared for the worst. Others packed up and hit I-75 headed north. We for some reason had a peace about staying and riding out the storm. As a matter of fact, many of our friends from other cities and countries offered us their homes and said if we needed a place to evacuate we could come to their home. We decided to stay put because for some reason the Holy Spirit kept confirming that everything would be OK. As we called around to make sure several of our leaders were OK, we had several who needed a place and we opened our home. Of those who came, one was our keyboardist and the other our worship leader. I began to ask God for instruction on how to proceed. The Lord gave us the instruction to do praise and worship in our home. We could hear the leaves blowing and the storm raging around us but we continued to praise God. As a result, many people who were in the midst of the storm tuned in to our live Facebook and Periscope broadcast.

The next morning when one of the news reporters made his report, he said, "Nothing short of a miracle occurred in Tampa last night. Someone must have been praying because Irma was stopped and collapsed in Tampa". A pastor friend of ours called and his wife said we believe that it was because of the suddenly prayers that believers in the city were impacted and that our city was saved. I too believe that the power of worship stopped a city from devastation. I believe that one or two believers gathering together in His name has the power to stop a hurricane. And if it can stop the same hurricane, which had destroyed other cities from destroying other ours, it has the same power to stop the storms in your life and produce a suddenly.

Our praise and worship just like that of Paul and Silas in the Philippian Jail has the ability to be a catalyst for breakthrough. Next time you get into a tough situation or a storm is headed your way, instead of worrying about it, create an environment of worship that lets God know you trust Him with your situation no matter how dark or tough it looks.

Prayer

Our next catalyst is prayer. There is a powerful result produced when believers come together in prayer. On numerous occasions we can see throughout Scripture that prayer produced the Suddenlies of God. Even in the text we just read pertaining to praise and worship where Paul and Silas were in jail we can see that prayer was also an ingredient in the occasion.

On one occasion in August 2017, during the Suddenly Conference in Davao City, Philippines, at Praise Revival Center my wife and I were in the midst of our Midnight Cry prayer and we felt the earth shaking. We were in the midst of an earthquake. We never stopped praying and although it was a fairly strong earthquake we didn't see any damage or any problems in the church.

Did you know that your prayer has the power to move mountains, open prison doors, and break chains. I love the story of the apostle Peter being held in prison in the Book of Acts.

> *Peter therefore was kept in prison: but prayer was made without ceasing of the church unto God for him. And when Herod would have brought him forth, the same night Peter was sleeping between two soldiers, bound with two chains: and the keepers before the door kept the prison. And, behold, the angel of the Lord came upon him, and a light shined in the prison: and he smote Peter on the side, and raised him up, saying, Arise up quickly. And his chains fell off from his hands. And the angel said unto him, Gird thyself, and bind on thy*

sandals. And so he did. And he saith unto him, Cast thy garment about thee, and follow me.

Acts 12:5-8 King James Version (KJV)

Again, we see the correlation between prayer and breakthrough. In this instance, we can also see the interweaving of unity. The church was praying and believing God for breakthrough for Peter and the angel of the Lord came and broke the chains and freed Peter from prison. Did you know that the Scripture says that when we pray if we believe that the things we say will come to pass that we will have them? I have learned to trust God for miraculous Suddenlies and have found that prayer is a tremendous catalyst for the Suddenlies of God.

I remember, when I was a young boy I had chicken pox. I was probably about 12 years old and we lived in the country parts of Arkansas. My grandmother had taken me to the doctor and they had given me some medicine and for whatever reasons it was taking its sweet time working. So I got the bright idea of putting water on my face and scratching the sores. Well unfortunately, it didn't work and had quite the adverse effect. Instead of it helping, it made things worse. The sores began to bleed and eventually scabbed up. The scabs were all around my mouth to the extent that I wasn't even able to eat. It was close to Thanksgiving and although Thanksgiving dinner was smelling extremely good I couldn't open my mouth wide enough to eat. I remember praying and asking God to please heal me so that I could eat. Miraculously God did just that, my scabs cleared up and I was able to open my mouth. My grandmother asked me what did I do and my response was, "I prayed." For years, she would say that there was something special about me, because when I prayed God always answered.

Did you know that just as I prayed and believed God for breakthrough and Suddenlies and God answered, He will do the same for you. We are praying for you that today you will experience a new dimension of prayer where your prayers are answered like never before.

Fasting

Although I love all the catalysts, this one catalyst has proven to be the most beneficial in our lives. We've seen more breakthroughs happen because of a lifestyle of fasting than anything else. One of the texts that speaks the loudest as it pertains to this topic can be found in Isaiah 58:8 wherein it says, "Then shall thy light break forth as the morning, and thine health shall spring forth speedily: and thy righteousness shall go before thee; the glory of the Lord shall be thy reward."

The text shares with us that when we fast in accordance with God's original intent for fasting that God would literally cause us to breakthrough. The Suddenlies of God manifest when we begin to pray and really subdue our flesh. I always like to caution believers that fasting doesn't move God it moves us into alignment with the heartbeat of God for our life and as such produces the manifestation of the things we have been believing for.

In 2007, Valora was given up to die. The doctors diagnosed her with an inoperable brain tumor and as a result they released her to go home and die. At the time, she was probably only 90 pounds. She had become so emaciated that they had to give her liquid fat. People from the church were praying and believing for her full recovery but it appeared it wasn't getting better. She remembered a story her grandmother had told her years before about a similar situation. Her grandmother too had been given up to die with a diagnosis of cancer. Doctors had given her less than 3 months to live. She refused to believe the doctors' report and she began a 40-day fast. She said that if she was going to die anyway she would at least give God a chance to heal her first. After the 40 days, she returned to the doctor and they found that the cancer was completely gone. She lived an additional 30 something years and when she died, it was not of cancer. She was an amazing woman whose faith in her God was coupled with fasting and it produced an amazing suddenly for her.

When Valora remembered her grandmother's testimony, she immediately applied this principle. She began to fast. She began to listen to the Scriptures on CD and pray as she fasted. In no time at all, her health began to get better and before she knew it, she returned to the doctor and the tumor was gone. Fasting was a powerful catalyst for breakthrough in her health.

I remember reading the book, "The Heavenly Man" which chronicles the story of a pastor in China who fasted and prayed for a year for a Bible. He determined to only eat one bowl of rice for that year and as a result at the end of the year a man appeared at his door bringing him a Bible. The next testimony he had was that he was in prison for preaching the Gospel and he fasted for over 90 days. Each day he would give his food to the other prisoners and at the end of the fast an angel came and escorted him out of the prison. He said, like Peter he thought it was a dream, but it wasn't, it was real.

Faith

Do you believe that your faith can actually move a mountain? I do! I believe that God's Word is impenetrable, infallible, and literally incapable of failure. One of my favorite Scriptures comes from Mark 11: 20-23. Here's what it says,

> *And in the morning, as they passed by, they saw the fig tree dried up from the roots. And Peter calling to remembrance saith unto him, Master, behold, the fig tree which thou cursedst is withered away. And Jesus answering saith unto them, Have faith in God. For verily I say unto you, That whosoever shall say unto this mountain, Be thou removed, and be thou cast into the sea; and shall not doubt in his heart, but shall believe that those things which he saith shall come to pass; he shall have whatsoever he saith.*
>
> *Mark 11:20-23 King James Version (KJV)*

For some people this may not even be impossible but I have seen first-hand what believing God by faith can do in any situation. One time in my life, I was facing a very tough legal battle. I had been sentenced to 20 years in the Tennessee Department of Corrections. One day I read this Scripture and it just leaped off the page. When I read the Scripture that day it, wasn't just another Scripture, but it actually produced life for me. I began to believe what it said. It was said that I would be 47 when I was released because there was no way I would be released earlier. I refused to believe that this was my end in life. I refused to believe that although I had not done everything correct in life that God was done with my life. I began to pray and fast and believe God by faith that He had the ability to move my mountain. The odds were against me. I had no money, I had no family to help, all I had was faith. As a matter of fact, my testimony is that my mother has been incarcerated all my life, my biological father I've never met, my oldest sister was killed at 33, my youngest brother was killed on a basketball court at 23, and my next oldest brother was killed in a drive by at 28. I've been alone most of my life but one thing I've always been able to depend on was God and His unfailing love for me. For me it produced a faith in Him that was unstoppable. As a result, after 4.5 years the sentence which had been once handed down in my case was overturned and reversed. Suddenly, what looked like there was no way out of was now removed out of my way. I walked into the courtroom the judge says, "Mr. Cole, It appears that we have made a mistake and that we will be releasing you." The next day I was leaving and going home after 4.5 years. This had only happened to 2% of the people in the history of the State of Tennessee Department of Corrections where someone's sentence had been overturned.

It was at this point in my life that I realized God had given me a gift of faith which when used always caused breakthrough in my situation. When the legal battle was won someone asked me what was my legal precedent. Most cases are either won or lost because of a legal standing or precedent. I smiled and said, "my legal precedent was Mark 11: 20-23."

The question you must ask yourself today is what will you have faith in God for? Will you trust Him or will you place more faith in what your circumstances say or what your fears say than you will what God is saying to you?

I remember in 1996, my grandmother was rushed to the hospital due to having had two heart attacks and a stroke. She was in a coma and I was stationed in the military in Schofield Barracks, Hawaii. They called for me to come home preparing for a funeral. I packed my bags and boarded the airplane for the 9-hour flight to Arkansas. When I landed in Memphis, Tennessee, my older sister came to pick me up and shared with me that my grandmother was probably not going to recover from the coma. As we neared the hospital, I asked God that he anoint me to pray for her. We arrived and got out of the car to walk in to the hospital and I could feel that God was going to do something amazing. She was in the ICU and of course we had to wash our hands and prepare to go into the room wearing isolation or protective gowns. When I walked into the room, my heart sank. I had never seen her like this, she was almost unrecognizable. The tears began to well up in my eyes as I held her hand. She was unresponsive. I leaned over to kiss her and I spoke to her and said I am here, your baby boy is here and you are going to be OK. I told her I loved her and I began to pray for her. As I began to pray, I could feel her hand squeeze and her eyes flutter. She knew I was there. 14 days later she was talking and walking and later went home without any signs of a stroke or a heart attack. We believe by faith that there is nothing too hard for God and that no matter how difficult or how impossible your situation looks there is nothing too hard for God. Today we decree that just as God has done the seemingly impossible for us, He will do it for you. No matter where you are or what you are facing we decree that the Suddenlies of God will manifest in your life. God is not done with you; neither is your situation so bad that He cannot turn it around. He loves you with an unquenchable love and He will not fail you so put your faith in Him and know that He is about to turn it around for your good.

Giving

The last catalyst we will discuss will be that of giving. The Scripture says that if we give, it shall be given unto us, pressed down shaken together and running over shall men given unto our bosom. I am a living witness that this Scripture will come to pass in the life of a person who believes God for breakthrough financially.

Once God challenged me to not only give my tithe of 10% but to double it for 24 months. So, for 24 months I sacrificed and gave the 20%. As a result, at the end of the 24 months God gave me a vision of starting a website design company. When I stepped out by faith and began to have meetings to develop the company the only challenge was finances. God reminded me that I had sowed by obedience not even knowing what the result would be. One day as I was driving with a friend of mine who was strong prophetically he turned to me and said, "You will meet a man not too many days from now who will give you the money for your business". I looked at him and said OK, if you say so I believe it. In less than 3 weeks, one day a young man walked up to me and said the Lord had told him to give me the money I needed to get my business started. Suddenly, God manifested what he said He would.

We have countless stories of people sowing a seed by faith and all of a sudden going to the mailbox and finding checks in the mail. Numerous testimonies are evident of people who gave an offering by faith and as a result they experienced supernatural provision. Several people in particular were amazed by God because they received checks from employers with whom they had worked years before and had changed addresses with no forwarding address. Valora and I received a check from BMW for a vehicle we had payed off and all of a sudden they sent us a check in the mail.

Recently, we were ministering in Detroit, Michigan, and we asked everyone to give an offering. One young lady in particular said she had come and didn't have any money at all. She looked into her PayPal and found that there was only $3.00. She said she quickly went in and sowed the seed online on the church's website and before she left she checked her business account and she said that there was 40 times what she had given.

We love to hear the testimonies of people who believe God and experience financial Suddenlies. You too can experience the sudden breakthrough in the area of your finances if you can trust God beyond what you can see. So get ready to experience God in your finances as you apply the catalyst of sowing like you never have before. Get ready for sudden financial breakthrough.

Chapter 8
Suddenly Confessions

Death and life are in the power of the tongue and they that love it shall eat the fruit thereof.

Proverbs 18:21

This is your Season of Sudden Breakthrough!

PROVERBS 18:21 DECLARES that "Death and Life are in the power of the tongue and that they who love it shall eat the fruit thereof." This text helps us to understand the power of the tongue and the power of speaking what we believe.

We remember a friend who shared with us about the difference between reading Scripture silently and reading it aloud. Some people may not think praying aloud will make a lot of difference but there is an important key given to us in Romans 10:17, which says, "Faith cometh by hearing and hearing by the word of God."

One of the key benefits to saying your declarations louder is that you begin to hear them yourself. As you hear the Scriptures over and over, they will begin to sink into your spirit and as your spirit is saturated with the Word of the Lord and faith, you become a prime candidate to receive the

Suddenlies of God. So, make it a priority to say these declarations several times a day so that they get into your spirit and as this happens, your faith will be strengthened.

Remember, your faith is like any other muscle and it takes proper nutrition and exercise to build muscle. A constant diet of Scripture and a constant exercise regime of faith will quickly put you into a place where you are filled with the power of God and enough faith to believe God for miracles in your life and the lives of those around you.

We remember a story of a mule that fell into an old dug well. The owner couldn't get him out so he decided to bury him there. However, what the old farmer didn't know was, as he was shoveling in the dirt, the old mule was shaking the dirt off and packing it under his feet. Before he knew it, the old mule was stepping out of the well. Just as it was with the old mule, if you build your muscle by declaring the Word of God daily, you will find that you too will come out of every circumstance, which has attempted to bury you.

Allow us to give you one more story, which reiterates the need to build your faith. There was a frog that fell into a hole and couldn't get out. When he fell in, his friends gathered around the top of the hole and began to tell him there was no use for him to try to get out because it was going to be impossible. Despite their yelling, he kept jumping and jumping and although on the first jump he didn't get out, it came to pass after a while that he jumped out of the hole. When he finally got out, his friends asked him why he hadn't responded to them and he said, "I couldn't hear you."

What they didn't know was that each time he jumped his leg muscles got stronger and stronger. Before he knew it, his leg muscles had gotten so strong that they propelled him up out of the hole. The moral to the story is that all things are possible with God. If you build your faith as a muscle and feed it Scripture, you will find yourself having the strength to overcome any and every obstacle in your life.

So, make it a commitment to make these declarations out loud several times a day until they have saturated your spirit and built your faith.

Confessions, which Release your Sudden Breakthrough

Let's Confess

Everything in my life is about to immediately, straightway, abruptly, without notice, and SUDDENLY change!

- Suddenly I will experience FAVOR!
- Suddenly I will experience INCREASE!

- Suddenly I will BREAK THROUGH every barrier and obstacle!

- Suddenly I will experience HEALING! Let every broken, bruised, and hurt place in my life be healed Suddenly, Immediately, Abruptly, Without Notice in Jesus Name!

- Suddenly I will receive new VISION! I will look past my current situation and see what God said about me before I was formed in my mother's womb! What I see with my natural eyes is subject to change SUDDENLY!

- Suddenly I am anointed with CREATIVITY! God, I believe you will give me one witty invention, one creative idea, which will SUDDENLY change my situation! Lord I thank you for the Anointing of Creativity because I am ready for my SUDDENLY!

- Suddenly I will experience EXPANSION! This is the season where God will suddenly expand my territory! I've been faithful over a few things now I am prepared to be ruler over much. Mega is my portion! Let it come Suddenly!

- Suddenly I will encounter supernatural CONNECTIONS! Let every connection I need for my next level come suddenly! Let Cornelius Connections, Divine Interactions, Divine Encounters, and Divine Intersections be my portion SUDDENLY in Jesus Name!

- Suddenly everything which has been held up will be RELEASED unto me! Let everything that has been held up, kept back, stagnant, and behind time in my life be released Suddenly! Let this be a time where the floodgates and heaven Suddenly open for me!

- Suddenly I will experience ACCELERATION! Let there be acceleration in my life SUDDENLY! I will go from a standstill to full speed Suddenly!

- Suddenly I will experience the STRENGTH OF GOD! Let the Strength of the ox be upon me as I complete my assignment in the earth! I won't get weary, wear out or wear down before my time! I will have the strength to complete every assignment SUDDENLY!

- Suddenly RESOURCES are manifesting for me! Let this be a season where every resource I need to fulfill my assignment in the earth be released SUDDENLY! May every resource, provision, and need be met in my life SUDDENLY in Jesus name!

- Suddenly I will be brought into greater levels of EXPOSURE! I've been hidden until now, but let my gift make room for me! Let it bring me before great men! Let this be my season of exposure! I shall go forth, let greater visibility be my portion SUDDENLY!

Chapter 9
Suddenly Declarations for Sudden Breakthrough

Thou shalt also decree a thing, and it shall be established unto thee and the light shall shine upon thy ways.

Job 22:28

SUDDENLY GOD IS releasing everything you have been believing for. Wait on it, expect it, don't blink, and Suddenly, what you have been praying for will manifest! Everything in your life is about to shift! Get ready, because as you make these declarations, you will be framing the atmosphere in which you live. Remember, we never speak that which we see, we only speak what God's Word says and that which we are believing for.

Just as confessing the Word brings great results, so does declaring it. Kings make declarations and when they go out, it is illegal for it not to prosper. Therefore, because you are an heir and a joint heir, your decrees are powerful.

Let's Decree

- Let vindication and justice be my portion SUDDENLY!

- Let everything that's been held up in my life SUDDENLY be released!

- Let every stagnant place in my life SUDDENLY accelerate!

- Let every barren place SUDDENLY flourish!

- Let every closed womb SUDDENLY open!

- Let every place where my soul is troubled, I will SUDDENLY experience the peace of God that passes all understanding!

- Let every underdog SUDDENLY be promoted!

- Let sickness and infirmity be SUDDENLY healed in every area of my life!

- Let marriages *SUDDENLY* be restored!

- Let every scale upon my eyes be removed *SUDDENLY* and let clarity of vision come forth!

- Let sinners be saved *SUDDENLY!*

- Let broken relationships be reconciled *SUDDENLY!*

- Let dry bones *SUDDENLY* live in Jesus Name!

- Let every desert in my life be turned into an oasis *SUDDENLY*!

- Let every naysayer and mocker be *SUDDENLY* confounded by my Success!

- Let my enemies *SUDDENLY* be scattered!

- Let my finances go from a trickle to a *SUDDENLY* overflow (the excess or surplus not able to be accommodated by an available space). Let there not be room enough to receive the blessings God is releasing in my life!

- Let my finances go from not enough to a *SUDDENLY* deluge (a severe flood; to inundate with a great quantity of something). Let there not be enough room!

- Let every addiction be broken now in Jesus Name! I am delivered and set free *SUDDENLY*!

- Let depression go *SUDDENLY* in Jesus Name!

- Let every weary person receive strength *SUDDENLY*!

- Let every no be turned into a yes *SUDDENLY*!

- Let every Red Light be turned Green *SUDDENLY*!

- Let Favor *SUDDENLY* be my portion in Jesus Name!

- Let every closed door be open *SUDDENLY* in Jesus Name!

- Let every tear be dried up *SUDDENLY* in Jesus name!

- Let my family member be saved *SUDDENLY* in Jesus name!

- Let my children be saved *SUDDENLY*!

- Let *SUDDENLY* come upon me, overtake me, and consume me!

- Let your faith arise *SUDDENLY* and speak for me!

Let's Decree

- Let your perspective *SUDDENLY* change! I will see what God sees and say what He said about me and my situation!

- Let hope be *SUDDENLY* restored in Jesus Name!

- Let deposits *SUDDENLY* be my portion!

- Let every plot, plan and scheme of the enemy against my life be rendered null and void SUDDENLY!

- Let your prophetic flow *SUDDENLY* catch fire!

- Let my gifts be *SUDDENLY* activated!

- Let the church have a burden *SUDDENLY* for souls!

- Let love *SUDDENLY* destroy hate and anger!

- Let a love revolution *SUDDENLY* be released in the earth!

- Let every empty place in my life and heart *SUDDENLY* be filled with the love of God!

- Let evangelism be strong in the earth *SUDDENLY!*

- Let strong revelatory preaching return to the pulpits *SUDDENLY!*

- Let unity come *SUDDENLY* to the Body of Christ!

- Let every wall and barrier to unity be brought down *SUDDENLY!*

- Let the peace that passes all understanding *SUDDENLY* overtake every worry in my life!

- Let the Finisher's Anointing be upon me *SUDDENLY*!

- Let sudden, uncontrollable, spontaneous worship break out in my church *SUDDENLY*!

- Let every spirit of procrastination go *SUDDENLY*!

- Let supernatural debt elimination come *SUDDENLY*!

- Let the double doors of success open *SUDDENLY*!

- Let promotion *SUDDENLY* come!

- Let minds be renewed *SUDDENLY*!

- Let every weary prophet come out of the cave and prophecy *SUDDENLY*!

- Let Jezebel and her whoredoms be thrown down *SUDDENLY*!

- Let every Absalom spirit planning a rebellion be overthrown *SUDDENLY*!

- Let every python spirit squeezing the life out of the people of God be uncoiled and destroyed *SUDDENLY*!

- Let every Korah attempting to lead rebellion be swallowed up *SUDDENLY*!

- Let every spirit of Leviathan, pride, high-mindedness, arrogance and self-centeredness be cast out *SUDDENLY*!

- Let stubbornness leave *SUDDENLY*!

- Let lust and perversion go *SUDDENLY*!

- Let religious spirits be overthrown by a genuine relationship *SUDDENLY*!

- Let anxiety go *SUDDENLY*!

- Let fear go *SUDDENLY*!

- Let intercessors come forth *SUDDENLY*!

- Let every power and principality that opposes my forward momentum be destroyed *SUDDENLY*!

- Let my mourning be turned to laughter *SUDDENLY*!

- And I shall sing and dance *SUDDENLY*!

- And I shall prosper *SUDDENLY*!

- And my harvest shall come forth *SUDDENLY*!

- And I will leap for joy *SUDDENLY*!

- And I will shout the victory *SUDDENLY*!

- And God shall do a new thing in my life *SUDDENLY*!

- Let every Saul spirit trying to assassinate me be uncovered and destroyed *SUDDENLY*!

- Let ever Miriam challenging my authority be removed *SUDDENLY*!

- Let the dew of Heaven *SUDDENLY* drop upon me and let it refresh me!

- Let the rain of God's provision fall *SUDDENLY*!

- Let the Glory of the Lord be upon me *SUDDENLY*!

- Let the Shekinah Glory overwhelm me *SUDDENLY*!

- The windows of heaven are opening *SUDDENLY* to make room for the blessings that have been poured out!

- Let my sphere of influence increase *SUDDENLY*!

- Let the Shamar (those that guard, preserve, and protect) Prophets get into position *SUDDENLY* and protect the church!

- Let the heavens open over me *SUDDENLY!*

- Let honoring one another be released *SUDDENLY!*

- Let forgiveness be released *SUDDENLY!*

Chapter 10

Prayer for Sudden Breakthrough

Be anxious for nothing but in everything by prayer and supplication with thanksgiving let your requests be made known unto God. And the peace of God, which passeth all understanding, shall keep your hearts and minds through Christ Jesus. Finally, brethren, whatsoever things are true, whatsoever things are honest, whatsoever things are just, whatsoever things are pure, whatsoever things are lovely, whatsoever things are of good report; if there be any virtue, and if there be any praise, think on these things.

Philippians 4:6-8

PRAYER IS A powerful tool, which yields great results in the life of the believer. Scripture declares that the fervent effectual prayer of the righteous avails much. Another translation would tell us that it has much power.

Here are basic principles for prayers that release suddenly.

1. Pray according to the Word of God

The Angels hearken to those who speak the Word of God.

> *Bless the Lord, ye his angels, that excel in strength, that do his commandments, hearkening unto the voice of his word.*
>
> *Psalm 103:20*

God watches over His Word to perform it.

> *Then said the Lord unto me, "Thou hast well seen, for I will watch over My word to perform it."*
>
> *Jeremiah 1:12*

It is the Word of God, not our words, which is sharper than a two-edged sword.

> *For the word of God is quick, and powerful, and sharper than any two-edged sword, piercing even to the dividing asunder of soul and spirit, and of the joints and marrow, and is a discerner of the thoughts and intents of the heart.*
>
> *Hebrews 4:12 (KJV)*

It is the Word of God that will not return void, not ours.

So shall my word be that goeth forth out of my mouth; it shall not return unto me void, but it shall accomplish that which I please, and it shall prosper in the thing whereto I sent it.

Isaiah 55:11 (KJV)

2. Couple your prayer with Faith

For verily I say unto you, that whosoever shall say unto this mountain, be thou removed, and be thou cast into the sea; and shall not doubt in his heart, but shall believe that those things which he saith shall come to pass; he shall have whatsoever he saith, **"When your faith is weak, couple it with fasting."** *(Remember fasting does not move God, however it does move our flesh, mind, will and emotions into a place of obedience and obedience moves the hand of God.)*

Mark 11:23 (KJV)

And Jesus said unto them, *"Because of your unbelief, for verily I say unto you, if ye have faith as a grain of mustard seed, ye shall say unto this mountain, "Remove hence to yonder place," and it shall remove. And nothing shall be impossible unto you.*

However, this kind goeth not out but by prayer and fasting."

Matthew 17:20-21 (CKJ - KJ21)

Let's Pray!

Father, in the mighty name of Jesus, I stand upon the authority of Your Word and I decree and declare that this is my Suddenly Season. I stand on the authority of Your Word, that according to Matthew 18:18-19, that where two or three are gathered in Your name, there You will be in our midst and that if two or three of us will touch and agree concerning the things that we ask, we shall receive the things we ask for. According to John 14:14, You said that if I ask anything in Jesus name, that You will do it that Your Father might receive the Glory.

Mark 11:21 declares that if I say unto the mountain, be thou removed and be thou cast into the sea and shall not doubt in my heart but shall believe, I shall receive the things I pray for. I shall have what I say. James 1:6 declares that a double-minded man is unstable in all his ways and such man should not expect to receive anything from You. I am not double-minded and I will stand firmly, relying in You and Your Word. I believe that You love me and that it is Your good pleasure to give me the Kingdom. So today, I declare this is my

Suddenly Season! It is the season where I will experience breakthrough in every area of my life and it shall be Suddenly. According to Isaiah 54:17, no weapon formed against me shall prosper and every tongue that rises up against me in judgment, I shall utterly condemn, for this is the heritage of the saints and my righteousness is of You. I believe that there is nothing too hard for You and that all things are possible to them that believe.

I realize that according to Proverbs 18:21, Death and Life are in the power of the tongue and they that love it, shall eat the fruit thereof. I choose to speak life. I choose to confess good things over my life, I choose to receive the end of my faith, which is breakthrough and success in every area of my life. I choose to believe Your report for my life. I will rejoice in You Lord and the Power of Your might. I declare this is the day that You have made and I will rejoice and be glad in it.

I know that You are my shield and my buckler and that even when my mother, father, and friends forsake me, You will take me up. I believe, without doubting that this is my Suddenly Season. This is the season where every prophetic promise You have given me, shall manifest. This is the season where my light shall spring forth Suddenly and my light shall spring forth as the noonday. I believe that now is the time that my cronos meets with Your Kairos and as they intersect, I shall experience suddenly after suddenly in my life. Prison doors shall open, healing shall spring forth, marriages shall be healed, relationships shall be reconciled, faith, strength, and passion for ministry and things that pertain to You shall be renewed, reset, and restored.

This is my appointed time to experience Your Suddenlies in my life because You are the God of the Suddenly! No good thing will be withheld from me because I am walking uprightly. I have delighted myself in You and I thank You that You are giving me the desires of my heart. I destroy every ideology and thought process, which is contrary to what Your Word declares about me. I pull down every stronghold in my mind, my flesh, or life, which is contrary to what You said about me and my destiny.

I lay aside every sin and weight, which has so easily beset me. I veto and cancel every assignment of the enemy formed against myself, my family, my marriage, my husband, my wife, my children, my sons, my daughters, my grandchildren, my nieces, my nephews, my church, my ministry, my business, my nonprofit, my city, my state, my country. I believe that when the enemy comes in like a flood, that You will lift up a standard against him and he is defeated. According to First John 5:14, I declare, that this is the confidence I have in You, if I ask

anything according to Your will, You hear me.
Because I know that You hear me in whatsoever I
ask, I know that I have the petitions that I desire of
You. Because I stand on the Word of God, it is
finished and completed in Jesus name.

Chapter 11

Suddenly Scriptures

IN THE BEGINNING of the book, we discussed several synonyms for the word suddenly: immediately, straightway, all of a sudden, abruptly, and without notice. In this section, we have included some of the most common texts that include either suddenly or one of its synonyms.

*And Hezekiah rejoiced, and all the people that God had prepared, for the thing was done **suddenly**.*

2 Chronicles 29:36

*Let all mine enemies be ashamed and sore vexed. Let them return and be ashamed **suddenly**.*

Psalms 6:10

*But God will shoot at them. They will be **suddenly** struck down with an arrow.*

Psalms 64:7

*I have declared the former things from the beginning and they went forth out of my mouth, and I shewed them. I did them **suddenly**, and they came to pass.*

Isaiah 48:3

Suddenly, *will my righteousness come near, and my salvation will be shining out like the light. The sea-lands will be waiting for me, and they will put their hope in my strong arm (BBE).*

Isaiah 51:5

Multitudes followed Him. And, behold, there came a leper and worshipped Him, saying, "Lord, if thou wilt, thou canst make me clean." And Jesus put forth his hand, and touched him, saying, "I will, be thou clean." And immediately, his leprosy was cleansed. And Jesus saith unto him, "See thou tell no man; but go thy way, shew thyself to the priest, and offer the gift that Moses commanded, for a testimony unto them."

Matthew 8:1-4

*And **suddenly** there came a sound from heaven as of a rushing mighty wind, and it filled all the house where they were sitting.*

Acts 2:2

*And **suddenly** there was a great earthquake, so that the foundations of the prison were shaken, and immediately all the doors were opened, and every one's bands were loosed.*

Acts 16:26

Straightway Scriptures

*But **straightway** Jesus spake unto them, saying, be of good cheer, it is I. Be not afraid.*

Matthew 14:27

*And **straightway** they forsook their nets, and followed Him.*

Mark 1:18

*And **straightway** the fountain of her blood was dried up; and she felt in her body that she was healed of that plague.*

Mark 5:29

*And **straightway** the damsel arose, and walked; for she was of the age of twelve years. And they were astonished with a great astonishment.*

Mark 5:42

*And **straightway** his ears were opened, and the string of his tongue was loosed, and he spake plain.*

Mark 7:35

***And one of the multitude answered and said**, "Master, I have brought unto thee my son, which hath a dumb spirit. **And wheresoever he taketh him**, he teareth him and he foameth, and gnasheth with his* teeth, and pineth away and I spake to thy disciples that they should cast him out, and they could not." He answereth him, and saith, "O faithless generation, how long shall I be with you? How long shall I suffer you? Bring him unto Me." **And they brought him** unto Him. And when He saw him, straightway the spirit tare him and he fell on the ground, and wallowed foaming.

And He asked his father, "How long is it ago since this came unto him?" And he said, "Of a child. **And oft times it hath cast him into the fire,** and into the waters, to destroy him, but if thou canst do anything, have compassion on us, and help us." **Jesus said unto him, "if thou canst believe, all things are possible to him that believeth."** And straightway the father of the child cried out, and said with tears, "Lord, I believe, help thou mine unbelief."

When Jesus saw that the people came running together, He rebuked the foul spirit, saying unto him, "Thou dumb and deaf spirit, I charge thee, come out of him, and enter no more into him." And the spirit cried, and rent him sore, and came out of him, and he was as one dead; insomuch, that many said, he is dead. **But Jesus took** *him by the hand, and lifted him up and he arose. And when he was come into the house, his disciples asked Him privately, "Why could not we cast him out?" And He said unto them, "This kind can come forth by nothing but by prayer and fasting."*

Mark 9:17-29

Immediately Scriptures

And, behold, two blind men sitting by the wayside, when they heard that Jesus passed by, cried out, saying, "Have mercy on us, O Lord, thou Son of David." And the multitude rebuked them, because they should hold their peace, but they cried the more, saying, "Have mercy on us, O Lord, thou Son of David." And Jesus stood still, and called them, and said, "What will ye that I shall do unto you?" They say unto Him, "Lord, that our eyes may be opened." So Jesus had compassion on them, and touched their eyes and immediately their eyes received sight, and they followed Him.

Matthew 20:30-34

And forthwith, when they were come out of the synagogue, they entered into the house of Simon and Andrew, with James and John. But Simon's wife's mother lay sick of a fever, and anon they tell Him of her. **And He came and took her by the hand,** *and lifted her up; and* **immediately** *the fever left her, and she ministered unto them.*

Mark 1:29-31

And there came a leper to him, beseeching Him, and kneeling down to him, and saying unto Him, "If thou wilt, thou canst make me clean." And Jesus, moved with compassion, put forth his hand, and touched him, and saith unto him, "I will, be thou clean." And as soon as He had spoken, immediately the leprosy departed from him, and he was cleansed.

Mark 1:40-42

And they come unto Him, bringing one sick of the palsy, which was borne of four. And when they could not come nigh unto Him for the press, they uncovered the roof where he was and when they had broken it up, they let down the bed wherein the sick of the palsy lay. When Jesus saw their faith, He said unto the sick of the palsy, "Son, thy sins be forgiven thee." But there were certain of the scribes sitting there, and reasoning in their hearts, "Why doth this Man thus speak blasphemies? Who can forgive sins but God only?" And immediately when Jesus perceived in His spirit that they so reasoned within themselves, He said unto them, "Why reason ye these things in your hearts? Whether is it easier to say to the sick of the palsy, Thy sins be forgiven thee; or to say, Arise, and take up thy bed, and walk? But that ye may know that the Son of man hath power on earth to forgive sins, (He saith to the sick of the palsy) I say unto thee, Arise, and take up thy bed, and go thy way into thine house." And immediately he arose, took up the bed, and went forth before them all; insomuch, that they were all amazed, and glorified God, saying, "We never saw it on this fashion."

Mark 2:3-12

*And his mouth was opened **immediately**, and his tongue loosed, and he spake, and praised God.*

Luke 1:64

***And he arose out of the synagogue**, and entered into Simon's house. And Simon's wife's mother was taken with a great fever, and they besought Him for her. **And He stood over her**, and rebuked the fever and it left her and **immediately** she arose and ministered unto them.*

Luke 4:38-39

And it came to pass, when He was in a certain city, behold a man full of leprosy, who seeing Jesus, fell on his face, and besought him, saying, "Lord, if thou wilt, thou canst make me clean." And He put forth his hand, and touched him, saying, "I will. Be thou clean." And immediately the leprosy departed from him.

Luke 5:12-13

And, behold, men brought in a bed, *a man which was taken with a palsy and they sought means to bring him in, and to lay him before Him. And when they could not find by what way they might bring him in because of the multitude, they went upon the housetop, and let him down through the tiling with his couch into the midst before Jesus. And when He saw their faith, He said unto him, "Man, thy sins are forgiven thee."* **And the scribes** *and the Pharisees began to reason, saying, "Who is this which speaketh blasphemies? Who can forgive sins, but God alone?"* **But when Jesus perceived** *their thoughts, He answering said unto them, "What reason ye in your hearts?* **Whether is easier, to say,** *Thy sins be forgiven thee; or to say, Rise up and walk?* **But that ye may know that the Son of man hath power**

upon earth to forgive sins, (he said unto the sick of the palsy,) I say unto thee, Arise, and take up thy couch, and go into thine house." And immediately he rose up before them, and took up that whereon he lay, and departed to his own house, glorifying God. **And they were all amazed,** *and they glorified God, and were filled with fear, saying, "We have seen strange things today."*

Luke 5:18-26

And a woman having an issue of blood twelve years, *which had spent all her living upon physicians, neither could be healed of any, came behind him, and touched the border of his garment and immediately her issue of blood stanched.*

Luke 8:43-44

And when the woman saw that she was not hid, *she came trembling, and falling down before Him, she declared unto Him before all the people for what cause she had touched Him, and how she was healed immediately.* **And he said unto her, daughter,** *be of good comfort, thy faith hath made thee whole, go in peace.*

Luke 8:47-48

And, behold, there was a woman which had a spirit of infirmity eighteen years, and was bowed together, and could in no wise lift up herself. And when Jesus saw her, He called her to him, and said unto her, "Woman, thou art loosed from thine infirmity." And He laid His hands on her and immediately she was made straight, and glorified God.

Luke 13:11-13

And it came to pass, that as he was come nigh unto Jericho, a certain blind man sat by the wayside begging. **And hearing the multitude pass by**, he asked what it meant. **And they told him**, that Jesus of Nazareth passeth by. And he cried, saying, "Jesus, thou Son of David, have mercy on me." **And they which went before rebuked him**, that he should hold his peace but he cried so much the more, "Thou Son of David, have mercy on me."

And Jesus stood, and commanded him to be brought unto Him and when he was come near, He asked him, saying, "**What wilt thou that I shall do unto thee?**" And he said, "Lord, that I may receive my sight." And Jesus said unto him, "Receive thy sight, thy faith hath saved thee." **And** *immediately,* he received his sight, and followed Him, glorifying God. And all the people, when they saw it, gave praise unto God.

Luke 18:35-43

And a certain man was there, which had an infirmity thirty and eight years. When Jesus saw him lie, and knew that he had been now a long time in that case, He saith unto him, "Wilt thou be made whole?" The impotent man answered him, "Sir, I have no man, when the water is troubled, to put me into the pool but while I am coming, another steppeth down before me." Jesus saith unto him, "Rise, take up thy bed, and walk." And immediately, the man was made whole, and took up his bed, and walked and on the same day was the sabbath.

John 5:5-9

And a certain man lame from his mother's womb *was carried, whom they laid daily at the gate of the temple which is called Beautiful, to ask alms of them that entered into the temple.* **Who seeing Peter and John about to go into the temple** *asked an alms. And Peter, fastening his eyes upon him with John, said, "Look on us." And he gave heed* unto them, expecting to receive something of them. Then Peter said, "Silver and gold have I none; but such as I have, give I thee. In the name of Jesus Christ of Nazareth, rise up and walk." And he took him by the right hand, and lifted him up and immediately, his feet and ankle bones received strength. And he leaped up, stood, and walked, and entered with them into the temple, walking, and leaping, and praising God.

Acts 3:2-8

And there he found a certain man named Aeneas, which had kept his bed eight years, and was sick of the palsy. And Peter said unto him, "Aeneas, Jesus Christ maketh thee whole. Arise, and make thy bed." And he arose immediately.

Acts 9:33-34

And at midnight Paul and Silas prayed, and sang praises unto God and the prisoners heard them. And suddenly, there was a great earthquake, so that the foundations of the prison were shaken and immediately all the doors were opened, and everyone's bands were loosed.

Acts 16:25-26

Chapter 12
Principles For Sudden Financial Breakthrough

GOD'S WORD GIVES us clear instructions concerning the importance of obedience. He has established principles, which we must apply to our lives in order to receive the blessing and financial breakthrough that He has already ordained for us. These principles, when applied, allow us to walk in financial freedom, which we will pass along to generations after us. We cannot plead the promises of God and violate His principles. We must establish priority concerning our finances. We must give to God first! This is the principle of tithing, in which you give God the first tenth of what He has blessed you with.

The purpose of tithing is to teach you to always put God first according to Deuteronomy 14:23. We should adhere to and follow after the vow of Jacob.

> **And Jacob vowed a vow,** saying, "If God will be with me, and will keep me in this way that I go, and will give me bread to eat, and raiment to put on. So that I come again to my father's house in peace, then shall the LORD be my God. And this stone, which I

*have set for a pillar, shall be God's house
and of all that thou shalt give me I will
surely give the tenth unto thee."*

Genesis 28:20-22

Our offering should show our appreciation to
God for His love, provision, and protection every
day. It is our demonstration to Him of the value and
worth we ascribe to Him.

*No man should appear before the Lord
empty handed. Each of you must bring a gift
in proportion to the way the Lord your God
has blessed you."*

Deuteronomy 16:16-17

We never want to be found guilty of robbing or
stealing from God by keeping the tithe and offering,
which belongs to Him. It is quite challenging to
steal from God and then ask Him to bless us.

Faithfulness in giving our tithes and giving
liberal offerings are minimum requirements, which
when we apply them in our lives will ensure that we
receive the financial breakthrough and harvest,
which rightfully belongs to all believers. When we
obey God's principles, God promises to open up
heaven over us and pour out a blessing that we
won't have room enough to receive. Giving to God
also includes our talent and our time. Our talent
represents our God-given ability and should be used

to advance the Kingdom of God by blessing others. We have to allot time to God in doing what He has called us to do. When we offer back to God, our time, talent, and treasure, what already belongs to Him, we are demonstrating that we are appreciative and grateful for all that he has blessed us with and it also prevents us from being selfish.

God loves a cheerful giver. We should be happy and excited when giving to God. Because God exceeds our expectation when He gives to us. We should purpose in our hearts to give God a large offering. When we sow big, we reap big; but when we sow small, we reap small.

> But this I say, He which soweth sparingly shall reap also sparingly; and he which soweth bountifully shall reap also bountifully. Every man according as he purposeth in his heart, so let him give; not grudgingly, or of necessity, for God loveth a cheerful giver. And God is able to make all grace abound toward you; that ye, always having all sufficiency in all things, may abound to every good work.
>
> *2 Corinthians 9:6-8*

We give to God, not because God is in need of something. We give to God because He requires us to give and it is our responsibility to give.

Everything that God created gives. It is His good pleasure to give to us. Remember we cannot plead the promises of God and dishonor His principles.

Closing

OUR PRAYER IS THAT you have been blessed by this book. If so, we would love for you to go onto our FB Fan Page and Amazon to leave a testimony of how the book blessed you. You can also browse through our joint Facebook page and see the videos from which the book was written.

We have also copied most of our 1:00 P.M. and 12:00 midnight Eastern Standard Time Periscopes and Facebook Live videos to our You Tube page as well.

May God continue to bless you with Suddenlies for all the days of your life as you apply His principles and seek after Him.

Reflections

List the areas where you are expecting the Suddenlies in your life.

_____

_____

_____

_____

_____

_____

_____

_____

_____

_____

_____

_____

_____

_____

_____

_____

_____

_____

_____

_____

_____

_____
_____
_____
_____
_____
_____
_____
_____
_____
_____
_____
_____
_____
_____
_____
_____
_____
_____
_____
_____
_____
_____
_____
_____
_____
_____
_____

_____
_____
_____
_____
_____
_____
_____
_____
_____
_____
_____
_____
_____
_____
_____
_____

Reflections

Find the 2-3 Scriptures which correspond to your needs for Suddenly.

_____
_____
_____
_____
_____
_____
_____

Sudden Breakthrough

118

_____

_____

_____

_____

_____

_____

_____

_____

_____

_____

_____

_____

_____

Reflections

Write out confessions, which correspond with your areas of Suddenly and confess them each day, 3 times a day for 21 days.

_____

_____

_____

_____

_____

_____

_____

_____

_____

_____

_____

_____

_____

_____

_____

_____

_____

_____

_____

_____

_____

_____

_____

_____

_____

_____

_____

_____

_____

_____

_____

_____

_____

_____

Reflections

_____

_____

_____

_____

_____

_____

_____

_____

_____

_____

_____

Reflections

Each day after you've meditated on the Scriptures and done your confessions and prayed, write down what you believe God is saying for at least 7 days.

Day 1

_____

_____

_____

_____

_____

_____

_____

_____

_____

_____

_____

_____

_____

_____

_____

_____

_____

_____

Day 2

_____

_____

_____

_____

_____

_____

_____

_____

_____

_____

_____

_____

_____

_____

_____

_____

_____

_____

_____

_____

_____

_____

_____

Day 3

_____

_____

_____

_____

_____

_____

_____

_____

_____

_____

_____

_____

_____

_____

_____

_____

_____

_____

_____

_____

_____

Day 4

_____

_____

_____

_____

_____

_____

_____

_____

_____

_____

_____

_____

_____

_____

_____

_____

_____

_____

_____

_____

_____

Day 5

_____
_____
_____
_____
_____
_____
_____
_____
_____
_____
_____
_____
_____
_____
_____
_____
_____
_____
_____

Day 6

_____
_____
_____
_____
_____

_____

_____

_____

_____

_____

_____

_____

_____

_____

_____

_____

_____

_____

_____

Day 7

_____

_____

_____

_____

_____

_____

_____

_____

_____

_____

_____

_____

_____

_____

_____

_____

_____

_____

_____

_____

_____

_____

_____

_____

_____

_____

_____

_____

_____

_____

_____

_____

_____

_____

_____

_____

_____

_____

_____

_____

_____

Reflections

Write down areas in your life which you know are enemies of your Suddenly Season, that is, fear, lust, anger, sin, procrastination, slothfulness.

_____

_____

_____

_____

_____

_____

_____

_____

_____

_____

_____

_____

_____

_____

_____

_____

_____

_____

_____

_____

_____

Reflections

Develop and write down your plan to destroy the enemies of your Suddenly Season.

_____

_____

_____

_____

_____

_____

_____

_____

_____

_____

_____

_____

_____

_____

_____

_____

_____

_____

_____

_____

_____

_____

_____

_____

Reflections

_____

_____

_____

_____

_____

_____

_____

_____

_____

_____

_____

_____

_____

Contact Us

We would love to hear from you. We are here to serve.

You can "Like" our pages on Facebook, Instagram, Twitter, and Periscope at:

www.facebook.com/perfectedlovetampa

www.facebook.com/lajunandvalora

www.periscope.com/lajuandvalora

www.instagram.com/lajunandvalora

www.twitter.com/lajunandvalora

You can also view our site to acquire teachings and other ministry products.

If you would like to sow into our ministry to help further the Gospel, please do so at www.lajunandvalora.com or via our mobile app on either Google Play Store or the Apple App Store under LaJun & Valora Cole.

MAILING ADDRESS

6720 East Fowler Avenue Suite 161 Temple Terrace, FL 33617

Telephone

(844) We-R-Cole 844-937-3653

Website

www.lajunandvalora.com

Email

info@lajunandvalora.com